IN PURSUIT OF THE
GOOD LIFE

IN PURSUIT OF THE GOOD LIFE

Strategies for Well-Being and Success in College

DUSTIN BRISSON

ROWMAN & LITTLEFIELD
Lanham • Boulder • New York • London

Published by Rowman & Littlefield
An imprint of The Rowman & Littlefield Publishing Group, Inc.
4501 Forbes Boulevard, Suite 200, Lanham, Maryland 20706
www.rowman.com

86-90 Paul Street, London EC2A 4NE, United Kingdom

Copyright © 2025 by Dustin Brisson

All rights reserved. No part of this book may be reproduced in any form or by any electronic or mechanical means, including information storage and retrieval systems, without written permission from the publisher, except by a reviewer who may quote passages in a review.

British Library Cataloguing in Publication Information Available

Library of Congress Cataloging-in-Publication Data Available

ISBN 979-8-8818-0100-7 (cloth : alk. paper) | ISBN 979-8-8818-0101-4 (ebook)

♾️™ The paper used in this publication meets the minimum requirements of American National Standard for Information Sciences—Permanence of Paper for Printed Library Materials, ANSI/NISO Z39.48-1992.

CONTENTS

Acknowledgments vii
Introduction ix

1	Why College?	1
2	Your Collegiate Self-Image	9
3	Overwhelming Opportunities	19
4	Choose Friends Patiently	29
5	Intrinsic Motivation	39
6	Busyness Is Not Productive	49
7	Effective Studying	57
8	Test Anxiety	65
9	Competitive Peers	75
10	Ask for Guidance	83
11	Grade Uncertainty	91
12	Course Planning	101
13	The Authentic Life	111
14	Uninteresting Courses	121
15	Deep Projects	129
16	After College?	139

Epilogue: Next Steps 149
Appendix: Philosophical Background 157
Notes 163
Bibliography 185
Index 205
About the Author 209

ACKNOWLEDGMENTS

My sincere thanks go to the many students who have provided encouragement and very helpful feedback on various drafts of this project. In particular, I am indebted to Andrew, Abby, Yi-An, Ellie, Himanshi, Ipsita, Makayla, Kevin, Shreya, Emily, Kevin, Becca, Ren, Julia, Jimmy, Rhoda, Megan, Silvi, Valeria, Rosemary, I'Deyah, Max, Serena, Emily, Shuyan, Benji, Lili, Viktoria, Erika, Fernando, Lilia, Julia, and Thea. Hopefully, they have gained as much benefit from the process as I have. Additionally, I would like to thank the intellectual giants whose contributions to modern philosophy and psychology run through this book, including Massimo Pigliucci, Gregory Lopez, Donald Robertson, William Irvine, Martin Seligman, and Angela Duckworth (I have had the pleasure of interacting with some of them).

INTRODUCTION

The purpose of higher education is to provide students with opportunities for self-improvement. The most obvious purpose of college is to provide students with the opportunity to acquire academic knowledge. In addition to being intrinsically valuable, this knowledge also prepares students for their future careers. Although rarely highlighted in the glossy brochures, the college experience also provides students with opportunities to identify and achieve their life goals, overcome adversity, develop communication skills, navigate group dynamics, strengthen their cultural awareness, and establish and apply a set of personal ethics. Taking advantage of these opportunities, however, can be challenging. The chapters in this book provide practical skills to maximize the benefits of higher education and be happy while in college. This book aims to help students pursue what Aristotle called "the Good Life," which is the state of prospering and living well through the cultivation of reason and intellect while enjoying a positive state of mind (see the appendix to this book).[1]

This book is organized around situations that commonly cause anxiety in undergraduate college students. In my experience, every student is negatively affected by each of the challenges discussed, although the severity varies from student to student and throughout the college experience. It is not a question of *if* a situation affects your life while in college, but *how much* it affects your life. Although several of the challenges described may not have reached problematic levels, learning and practicing can limit the negative impact so they never become significant concerns. In my experience, students find that the minimal effort involved in improving their life satisfaction and well-being is well worth making.

The approaches described in this book can reduce the negative impacts of situations that students often find challenging. These approaches provide a set of skills that will enable you to recast difficult situations as opportunities—to see difficulties as circumstances that work to your advantage—leading to both life satisfaction and academic success. For example, the approaches in chapter 8, "Test Anxiety," can help you to harness moderate test anxiety, which every student experiences to some extent, to motivate your studies and minimize test-day panic. These ideas will reduce the detrimental effects of test anxiety and enable you to use exams to aid your educational experience and personal growth. Each chapter provides similar types of ideas and practices to succeed academically while maintaining your well-being.

Practicing the approaches before encountering a challenging situation will limit the adverse effects these situations can have on your well-being. As an analogy, it is much more effective to practice the song you will play *before* performing it in front of an audience. Practicing during times of relative calm will prepare you for times when action is needed. When times are stressful, on the other hand, practicing is much more challenging, though still useful.

It is not difficult to understand the rationale and theory described in these chapters. In fact, many students find that some concepts seem obvious once they have read them. Each chapter presents relatively few concepts and can be read in less than twenty minutes. However, there is a crucial difference between understanding the underlying theory and learning to use the information to improve well-being, life satisfaction, and academic performance. The former can be accomplished quickly through minimal contemplation, whereas the latter requires intention and repetition. By analogy, learning the theory behind hitting a baseball or playing the piano does not propel one to the Major Leagues or Carnegie Hall without practice. Practicing the exercises described in this book helps students develop "muscle memory" to reduce the negative impacts of potentially tricky situations quickly and effectively (please see the epilogue for a limited catalog of titles focusing on the philosophical and academic foundations of these practices).

> *Well-being is attained little by little,*
> *and nevertheless is no little thing itself.*
> —ZENO[2]

HOW TO USE THIS BOOK

Each chapter discusses the causes and typical consequences of a common challenge students encounter in college. Each chapter also provides step-by-step solutions to leverage these situations to improve academic success in college, all while maintaining a positive state of mind. The opening paragraph features a narrative of a hypothetical student to illustrate how a common predicament reduces the likelihood of academic success and diminishes the well-being and life satisfaction of college students. Each narrative example is a composite of many real students with whom I have interacted. *No story is a biography of any individual student.*

The illustrative stories are followed by a brief overview of relevant research and teachings from ancient philosophy, modern psychology, and human evolutionary biology. Although some of the research supporting the theoretical foundations discussed is cited in the chapters, no chapter provides a comprehensive review of the relevant literature. In each chapter, quotes and teachings from writers, philosophers, academics, and others illustrate the ideas in the opening paragraph. Important note: I endorse only the ideas expressed in the quotes; I am *not* endorsing the person quoted, as some may have committed unsavory acts of which I am unaware.

The theoretical foundations are followed by practical guides that can be used to capitalize on the difficult circumstances that college students face. Each practice—derived from philosophy, modern psychology, and human evolutionary biology—has proven effective for some, but not all, students who have tried them. Practicing the exercises for about a week will allow you to evaluate their potential for improving *your* quality of life. A good strategy is to first read the entire chapter and reflect on the theory and the practical applications. Then use the next several days to practice the approaches. Before you move on to the next chapter, take a few minutes to contemplate the usefulness of the practices and how you might implement them to improve your life. I recommend using a separate journal or notebook to respond to the prompts where writing is recommended.

CHAPTER ONE

WHY COLLEGE?

With only 1.5 semesters remaining to complete her bachelor's degree, Sara finally admits to herself something she has known for years: she does not want to be a physician. Even though she earned solid grades in the premed track, Sara has not enjoyed a single course, and she dreads the prospect of five more years of medical training. Her lack of interest in the numerous premed courses she took during college has greatly diminished her college experience, her well-being, and her life satisfaction. Still, the college experience has not been all bad for Sara. During her time in college, she took several philosophy courses and enjoyed them all. She still reads Kierkegaard for fun and her philosophy professors told her she possesses both a passion and a talent for the subject. *It is too late for me to change my direction now*, she thinks to herself as she opens her anatomy textbook to yet another uninteresting topic, resigning herself to an unsatisfying life in a profession she detests.

> *What carest thou for what is whispered here?*
> *Follow thy path, and let the people talk!*
> —DANTE ALIGHIERI[1]

Stories like Sara's are unfortunately all too common. Why do so many students spend their young adult lives pursuing a life goal they dislike? Even though every student follows a different path, the factors that lead them to pursue an unsuitable academic path or career are often similar. In general, children and young adults are pressured to decide their future careers, despite having almost no experience in those fields or knowledge of how to succeed. Older adults ask kids and young adults some version of *"What do you want to be when you grow up?"* so often that it has become cliché. In this way, young people are forced to choose their career path and to announce it without any knowledge of that career or any other possible careers. The common supportive responses from these older adults—*"That's great"* or *"You're so smart"*—then make many young people feel that changing their career path will be viewed as a failure.

Most young people are not even asked what they want. For most people, their career decisions are made for them based on the expectations of their family and their community. In other words, many young people feel that they are expected to be a doctor because *"We are a family of doctors"* or they hear *"You're smart. You should be an engineer."* Continually examining and reexamining your ambitions is the best way to avoid pursuing unsuitable goals as Sara did. In spite of what others in your community may think, altering your goals to align with your passions will promote life satisfaction and is the opposite of failure.

According to cognitive science research, rationally examining and reflecting on your goals increases your chances of reaching those goals.[2] Examining your long- and short-term goals is essential for ensuring they align with your values and current desires. Importantly, the process of continuously reevaluating your goals allows you to make course corrections as you gain new information, which is crucial to achieving the goals you actually want.

Young people often form their goals and the routes to achieve them through opinions, comments, coercion, and outright commands from those they respect or fear such as their family, mentors, and friends.[3] The fact that we are initially guided by those who genuinely want to see us succeed is not problematic. Taking ownership of goals that are forced on us and believing that they are "my" goals, without questioning if these goals can result in well-being and life satisfaction in "my" life, is problematic. As writer Joseph Campbell advised, "If you can see your path laid out in front of you step by step, you know it's not your path."[4] It is not uncommon for people to follow a trajectory that is not right for them because they do not take the time to think if this is actually what they want. Further, people often choose not to change course—even when they realize that they are on a path that makes them miserable—in order to avoid disappointing their community. In their minds, changing course would be like admitting defeat or that they were wrong ("Oh, the horror!").

This chapter explores the goal you are currently pursuing—going to college. *Why are you going to college?* Students who are asked this question are likely to respond with something about the need for a college degree in order to achieve their career goals. Few students, however, consider this question in any detail. Even more surprising, almost no student is ever asked why they want to attend college. It is far more common that high school students will be asked "What college will you attend?" than "Why do you want to go to college?" To be clear, my intention is not to discourage you from continuing your education—far from it. In addition to career success, higher education is correlated with higher levels of well-being, life satisfaction, and enjoyment.[5] I am suggesting that you should take the time to ensure that you are psychologically and emotionally prepared to attend college. By making certain that you are attending college for the right reasons and at the right time, you will maximize the benefits of your educational journey. Identifying the reasons you want to attend college is the first step to achieving success and, more importantly, to being satisfied with your choices now and in the future.

PRACTICE AND APPLICATION

We are told what are and are not good choices throughout our adolescence and young adulthood. This guidance is almost always received after we engage in questionable activities resulting from questionable decisions. The guidance is rarely accompanied by an explanation of *why* the decision was "good" or "bad" except as it relates to consequences. Even though our parents and mentors were likely dedicated to developing our ethical decision-making skills, this type of guidance prepares us to make better choices in the future only when the exact same situation arises.

This type of guidance is not ideal if the goal is to learn how to make the most appropriate choices in novel situations. In this chapter, you will work on developing your decision-making framework by concentrating exclusively on information that increases the probability of arriving at the best decision for you. This simple framework is centered on two fundamental pillars of decision-making: decisions should aim to improve the quality of your life and should focus on achievable goals.

Quality of Life

A good decision is one that aligns with your pursuit of the good life. Decisions that aid in your pursuit of the good life, as defined by Aristotle,[6] result in actions that cultivate your intellect and ethical behaviors so that you can achieve success while maintaining a constant state of well-being. To align your decisions with your pursuit of the Aristotelian good life, you must deliberately think about the motivations and pressures affecting your decisions (see my definition of "the good life" in the appendix and chapter 5). Take a few moments to consider what has motivated you to attend college. For example, do you enjoy education and want to learn more? Do you think college is necessary to have a good career? Do you feel pressured by your parents or your peers? Does college just seem like what people do after high school, and you are just going along with expectations? Do you fear being judged as a failure if you do not attend college now? Use your notebook to address these prompts and any other motivations you may have for attending college now.

Good decisions are generally motivated by intrinsic factors such as life satisfaction and personal desires (see chapter 5). That is, motivation to engage in activities or behaviors simply because they are naturally satisfying to you. Internally motivated decisions tend to promote well-being, ethical behaviors, and many long-term benefits. Poor decisions, on the other hand, are often the result of extrinsic motivations, such as seeking external validation or avoiding criticism. Extrinsically motivated decisions may provide short-term relief from external pressures, but they are much less likely to promote long-term well-being and satisfaction (please refer to chapter 5 for a detailed discussion of intrinsic and extrinsic motivation). You may find it challenging to accept that your decisions should be motivated solely by intrinsic factors since most people use a mix of intrinsic and extrinsic motivations. According to current research, however, people who are exclusively intrinsically motivated have a heightened sense of well-being and are more successful academically and in their careers.[7]

Look over your responses and highlight those that are internally motivated—those that bring you satisfaction regardless of the views of others—and those that are influenced by external pressures. Actions propelled by external pressures may provide some temporary relief, but they will not lead to long-term satisfaction or personal well-being. In your notebook, write a brief description of what decision you might make if there were no external pressures. Although it is unlikely that you can completely eliminate external pressures, you will be better able to pursue the good life if you make decisions based on your internal motivations.

It is helpful to remember that your goals, and therefore your internal motivations, will change as you learn and grow. Revisit this exercise every few months to ensure that you remain on a path that is truly satisfying for you. When you make decisions based on your internal motivations, you greatly increase your chances of being successful and satisfied in college and of being successful and satisfied with the life you lead after college. The pursuit of the good life should result in life satisfaction and promote well-being now and in the future.

Achievable Outcomes

You should dream big. You should make decisions that will enable you to achieve great things while promoting your well-being and enhancing your quality of life. However, decisions that lead you toward attempting to achieve the unachievable will lower your feelings of well-being and life satisfaction and decrease your motivation to continue on that path. Achievable outcomes are those that are within your control and that you are intrinsically motivated to achieve. There is a tendency for students to focus on outcomes over which they have no control and that are, with respect to their decisions, unachievable. That is not to say these outcomes will not happen—they might—but your decisions cannot affect outcomes over which you have no control. For example, you have complete control over your efforts to become more knowledgeable, but you cannot control the desires or actions of your parents, mentors, or friends. As a result, a decision to attend college with the goal of self-improvement and learning (under your control) will always result in success and well-being, whereas a decision motivated by the goal to satisfy the desires of your parents (not under your control) is unlikely to result in success and may result in unnecessary suffering.

For the next exercise, revisit your motivations for attending college. That is, what are the reasons why you have chosen the path you are on? In your notebook, create a table like the example that follows. In the left column of the table, provide a brief description of your motivation for attending college; in the right column, describe the aspects, if any, that are within your complete control. By adjusting your motivations to focus exclusively on what you can control completely—the aspects that are readily achievable—you will be able to improve the quality of your decisions. You can improve both your probability of success in college and your well-being by intentionally considering your motivations now and throughout your college career.

MY MOTIVATIONS	ASPECTS UNDER MY CONTROL
To learn biology	My effort to learn biology is entirely within my control and depends only on my choices.
To earn good grades	I can influence my grades by learning the material but the grade itself is not in my control. Focusing on learning is my best chance at success and well-being.

PURSUIT OF THE GOOD LIFE

Keeping your motivations in mind is essential to making the choices that will lead to the greatest degree of academic success and life satisfaction. This chapter includes lessons and exercises that help you determine whether your decisions are based on your true desires or if they are driven by family and societal pressures. Good decisions that are well-motivated and attainable will result in life satisfaction and well-being now and in the future. Poor decisions, on the other hand, may ease some pressure now, but may lead to misery in the future. Sara, for instance, will successfully complete a major she hates, which will lead to a life she neither wants nor enjoys. Remember that just because you can achieve a goal does not mean that you should. Similarly, just because a decision is properly motivated does not mean it is a good choice if it is not achievable.

Every event in your life, including those in college, will expose you to new information that can change your goals and internal motivations. Regularly revisiting these exercises will allow you to adjust or change your trajectory in order to remain focused on goals that will promote your well-being, life satisfaction, and other measures of success. A word of caution: these lessons and exercises, like all lessons and exercises, work only if you practice them in good faith. That is, if you are motivated by a fear of failure, convincing yourself that quitting college will make you happier will not improve your well-being or life satisfaction. Identifying your true motivations, which requires effort and can be frightening at times, is essential to making good decisions.

KEY POINTS

- Goals and career paths are often dictated by comments from people who are respected or feared and not through a personal exploration of all options.
- Many people continue to follow unsatisfactory life paths because they never consider whether the path they are on is what they actually want or if they have assumed ownership of goals instilled by parents or other mentors.
- To many, changing course is admitting failure. However, altering your path to align with your passions promotes well-being and life satisfaction, the opposite of failure.
- Continuously reevaluating your goals allows for course corrections, which is crucial to achieving the goals you actually want to achieve and will promote life satisfaction and well-being.

CHAPTER TWO

YOUR COLLEGIATE SELF-IMAGE

Marcus has always been a "good student." Throughout his life, he was praised for his performance in the classroom, his volunteer work, and his athletic accomplishments on the tennis court. His image of himself as a good student was reinforced when he received an acceptance letter from his parents' alma mater, the university he had been dreaming of attending since childhood. His summer was filled with celebrations with friends and family, all of whom were excited about his future as a college student. Marcus was a "success," and he had the résumé and college acceptance letter to prove it. His core beliefs about himself were challenged, to put it mildly, during his first days on campus. He met many students whose accomplishments were at least as impressive as his own, and several were impossibly impressive. Further, it appeared that every other new student he met was perfectly prepared for their entire college experience; they had chosen a major, planned their course schedule for the first two years, knew which professors and courses to avoid, and knew what clubs and fraternities to join. Marcus could not even find his own room in the dorm. Without the core belief that he was a good student, he felt lost: who was he supposed to be if he was not more accomplished than his peers? After being praised regularly for his accomplishments in his small hometown, who is he now in an ocean of highly accomplished students?

> *Tranquility comes when you stop caring what they say, or think, or do.*
> —MARCUS AURELIUS[1]

It is a disconcerting realization for many new college students that they will no longer receive the kind of regular praise they were accustomed to in high school. The unanticipated realization that our core identity—how we define ourselves and view our place in the world—is incorrect can result in minor discomfort in the best-case scenario and an existential crisis in the worst case.[2] It is nearly universal for people to question their identities during times of transition, but it is not inescapable. The discomfort that arises from challenges to our core identity—often referred to as "self-image"—increases in proportion to our confidence that our self-image is an accurate and unchanging portrait of who we really are. An important question, then, is how we acquire our self-image in the first place. I expect that both Marcus and you would benefit by asking "How did I come to be defined as *successful*?" and "Why does this definition matter to me?"

Everyone, including Marcus, is constantly being defined by others. However, these "Definitions belong to the definer, not the defined."[3] People who know you well see you as an intricate and multifaceted individual. Nevertheless, their perceptions of you are a simplified version of how complex and dynamic you really are. In the minds of people who know you less well, your image is even more simplified and based on only one or a few characteristics or actions. For example, Marcus's tennis coach likely knows him only as a dedicated tennis player with little knowledge of any other aspect of his life. Such definitions can be helpful tools for your friends, family, and acquaintances, as they provide a point of reference for their interactions with you.

The fact that other people define you, or that you define others, is neither inherently good nor bad. However, allowing the definitions of others to shape your self-image has numerous negative consequences. Even so, many people allow praise and disapproval—especially from those they trust or admire—to shape their understanding of their own core identity, potentially to the point that they believe they *are* what others think they are.[4] Many of us understand who we are, at our very core, based entirely on the views and expectations of those around us. Throughout this chapter, you will learn how to loosen your grip on your static self-image without destroying your social network.

The way that you define yourself constrains the set of possible reactions, decisions, and future directions that are available to you.[5] Your actions—"*a good student like me* should study on Friday nights"—or your feelings—"*a kind person* would never get angry"—are governed by your understanding of your core identity. There is nothing intrinsically wrong with this. A fluid, well-examined self-image serves as a core organizing principle of our actions and develops continuously during our lives. Your self-image allows you to quickly identify the most appropriate course of action in any situation (see chapter 1). A static self-image, however, based on approval or disapproval from our parents, mentors, and friends, can be a prison that prevents personal growth. Holding tightly to a static self-image discourages self-exploration and prevents personal development. Developing an understanding of how praise and criticism have affected the core identities of humans throughout our social evolution enables you to understand what motivates the development and maintenance of your core identity and how it can be beneficial or detrimental.

Static self-images built on admiration from others need to be continually reinforced through praise.[6] For example, most of us have experienced a classmate who is obsessed with winning praise. These students never miss an opportunity to correct a classmate, to claim more than their share of credit for group projects, or to answer the professors' questions with other people's ideas. It is critical for these students to receive praise in order to maintain their self-image. You can rest assured that your professors are just as frustrated by these individuals as you are. Despite this, you may feel a hint of jealousy from the attention they receive.

Understanding why others seek praise and what they gain from these behaviors will alleviate any jealousy you may experience. Ask yourself, what is the true value of praise in their (or your) life? Praise can buy you no flour nor eggs and does not, on its own, make you more attractive. In the same way, you can investigate the many disadvantages of praise-seeking behaviors. Praise can temporarily boost feelings of well-being, but it is often followed by praise "withdrawals," which can lead to more aggressive praise seeking. That is, praise can be addictive.[7] In contrast, focusing on self-improvement, regardless of the recognition you may receive, adds value to your life with no disadvantages. Personal growth is entirely within your control and results in heightened well-being, increased life satisfaction, gratitude for the life you have, and, in many cases, as much flour and eggs as you can eat.[8]

Praise is associated with positive feelings such as love, affection, and interpersonal bonds, which have helped social species such as humans survive throughout evolutionary history. Moreover, praise plays a role in establishing and maintaining dominance hierarchies within social groups, in primates as well as some modern human societies, which determine access to the primary drivers of evolutionary success (i.e., food and mates).[9] However, social hierarchies based on the accomplishments of members create a constant need to seek recognition from others and an overwhelming sense of insecurity. Although our instinctual reactions to praise may have served our ancestors well, it is reasonable to question their value in our modern society. Do you truly believe your friends and family will desert you if you fail periodically? Do people like you because you are successful? The answers to these questions are an obvious and resounding *"no"* for the former and a less obvious but equally clear *"no"* for the latter. As an obvious side note, people who appreciate you only for your accomplishments believe that a connection to you can make them more successful but do not actually like or respect you. It does *feel* nice, though. Innumerable benefits will flow from unburdening yourself of the definitions about yourself that have been shaped by external praise, criticism, and expectations.

PRACTICE AND APPLICATION

Define Your Values, Not Yourself

We have described self-image as a deeply held set of definitions about who we are at our core. It would be more practical to view our core identity as *arising from* our core values rather than as a set of imposed definitions. Remember that it is rarely useful to *define* yourself. Definitions of you can benefit others by allowing them to quickly estimate what to expect from their interactions with you. You do not need a tool to quickly assess who you are or what to expect from interactions with yourself.

It is, however, useful to clearly define your core values. Your core values are guiding principles that allow you to differentiate right from wrong and to determine which behaviors and actions are appropriate in each situation. These values will continue to develop as you gain experiences throughout your life. Thus, evaluating and reevaluating your values will allow you to choose the best paths to reach worthwhile goals that are both attainable and that employ actions and behaviors you will not regret. To begin, take two to three minutes to describe three things that you desire in life. That is, write a brief description of your greatest dreams and wishes in your notebook.

Now take an additional two to three minutes to write three things in your notebook that you admire in three people whom you respect. In other words, what are the qualities, characteristics, and behaviors of these people you respect? You do not need to know the person well, nor does the person need to be a saint or even a real person. Simply focus on the qualities, characteristics, and behaviors you admire.

This list of attributes that you admire is a much more accurate representation of your core values than your list of desires. For many of us, the things we most admire in other people do not match the things we most desire for ourselves. The desired-versus-admired divergence suggests that you may be actively putting energy and effort into becoming someone who does not share your values. Now take three to five more minutes to write down a few additional qualities, characteristics, or behaviors to the list of traits that you most admire about humanity or about specific people.

Congratulations on completing the first draft of your core values. Hopefully this is the first draft of hundreds of future revisions. You should evaluate and reevaluate your core values regularly to ensure that they guide your daily actions and behaviors and to update them as you learn and gain experience. Your decisions should be guided by these values and not by a static image of yourself.

Making the Most of Praise and Criticism

A consistent and sustained effort will be required to diminish the influence of past praise and criticism on your self-image. An even greater effort will be required to reduce your desire for praise and aversion to criticism. Regardless of how much effort is necessary, these practices will yield positive results.

Praise and criticism are detrimental to your progress and well-being if you value the reassurance derived from praise or avoid the discomfort from criticism. However, the *information* contained within the praise and criticism can be valuable to your progress and should not be ignored. The opinions of others, especially those who have the relevant expertise or experience, are important guides for your personal growth, education, and even your values. It will take practice to internalize the distinction between the beneficial information contained in praise and criticism and the destruction that praise and criticism can impose on your self-image and core values. Two primary exercises can be used to leverage the opinions of others for your personal progress without allowing these opinions to corrupt your core values.

- *Separate your emotional response to the praise or criticism from the information contained within the opinion.* The value of the information can then be accurately assessed without the interference of an emotional response.
- *Evaluate the person giving the information.* Is their opinion sufficiently well-informed, based on their expertise or experience, regarding you or the subject matter? What motivates them to express their opinions? Is their value system compatible with yours? Recognizing that you are also imperfect and prone to errors can also help you to separate your emotional and rational responses to their opinions.

To begin, write a brief description of a recent event in which you felt either praised or criticized in your notebook.

Separate Your Rational Thoughts from Your Emotions

Take a deep, calming breath and recognize that this praise or criticism is not about you as a person. In fact, it likely reflects more about the person expressing the opinion than it does about you. Allowing yourself a moment of pause will permit you the space to observe your emotional state more objectively and to separate your rational thoughts from those driven by your emotional reaction. It is important to note that you should *not* suppress or avoid your emotions—emotions are a vital part of life—it is also important to not let your emotions control your decisions and actions. In your notebook, describe your *feelings* regarding the praise or criticism outlined above. Feel free to use single words or longer stories; it is very challenging to describe feelings in words.

Now outline in writing why you might give your friend similar praise or criticism. That is, what you would like your friend to understand if you gave the same praise or criticism.

Evaluate the Information within the Praise or Critique

You can assess the value of praise or criticism by distancing your emotional reaction from your rational thoughts. The first step is to assess the expertise and motivations of the person providing the opinion. If the person has no experience with the subject or the opinion is meant to be destructive, then the opinion is unlikely to be useful. If their opinion is not useful, you can safely disregard it. It should not bother you if another person acts incorrectly or foolishly, and it does not benefit you to engage with them when they do. *Warning:* Reflexively focusing on the negative characteristics of the person providing the opinion is appealing but can be counterproductive. You might feel better temporarily when you react this way, but you risk dismissing valuable information. For this exercise, focus on whether the person giving the opinion has appropriate expertise and is trying to be constructive, not on personal shortcomings.

Once you have determined that the person has some expertise and is acting in good faith, the second step is to place the opinion within the appropriate context. That is, determine how the information contained in the opinion can be beneficial to your life. In your notebook, describe how the praise or criticism you described above could be valuable to you and how you could use that information to guide your personal growth, values, education, or other type of success.

You now have a foundation to use the information derived from praise or criticism constructively and to your benefit. It will take practice to apply this technique, especially the initial step of separating your emotional reaction from your rational assessment of the information. To practice over the next several days, I suggest applying this exercise to one or two events from your past in which you felt praised and one or two in which you felt criticized. This technique is an effective tool to handle praise or criticism that, in your past, may have had a large and negative impact on your well-being.

Opportunities, Not Obstacles

There is a reason why you went to college. The college experience provides opportunities for personal growth in addition to a great education and a chance to make lifelong friends. Personal growth, by definition, requires a change in your self-image or core values. Participating in opportunities that could expand or alter your self-image will be arduous and extremely uncomfortable if you have a crystallized self-image. Furthermore, this discomfort will hinder your persistence, preventing you from benefiting fully from the opportunities. By acknowledging that you are continuously changing and improving, you will be able to accurately evaluate the value of opportunities and utilize them to their fullest.

Mentally reframing obstacles as opportunities will allow you to discover the benefits of any situation. College opportunities are like open doors that you can pass through if you work hard enough. The way you approach these opportunities, by either focusing on the open door (the benefit) or on the difficulties of passing through it (the obstacle), will determine the extent to which you can utilize these opportunities and how they affect your sense of well-being and satisfaction.

Use your notebook to describe a challenging situation you have faced or will face in the near future. Regardless of the actual outcome, describe what you believe is the best possible outcome that could result, or could have resulted, from the event. Describe how that can or could impact your life in a positive way (i.e., how you could become a better or more knowledgeable person as a result).

Now briefly describe in writing what you believe to be the worst possible outcome that could result from the event. Take a deep and calming breath to help provide some emotional distance and write only the facts about the situation.

Now describe how this "worst possible outcome" can or did make you a better or more informed person. Although this can be very challenging, I expect that you can find at least one benefit from this scenario.

You may recognize this approach from modern mindfulness and positive psychology. The point is that every situation can promote self-improvement when viewed from the right perspective. As with all approaches, this will take practice, especially in gaining enough emotional distance to identify the positives in any situation. You may wish to revisit this difficult situation over the next few days in order to gain additional emotional distance and to identify additional opportunities for self-improvement. As a bonus, write a note about how your well-being improves each time you revisit this situation.

PURSUIT OF THE GOOD LIFE

College offers many opportunities for self-improvement in areas such as work ethic, interpersonal skills, life philosophy, and academics, among others. Taking full advantage of these opportunities requires a flexible self-image. Although you cannot control how others define you, you can control how their opinions and expectations affect how you view your core identity. Additionally, you can learn to utilize the information in praise and criticism for self-improvement without allowing the praise or criticism to negatively affect your well-being or your core identity. Assessing and reassessing your core identity is the best approach to ensure that your values are, in fact, *your* values. Continuously reevaluating your values also reinforces the idea that your core identity develops continuously throughout your life. Accepting and appreciating positive changes to your self-image will enable you to make the most of the opportunities that college provides in your pursuit of the good life. It takes courage and practice to live according to your core values and is discussed throughout this book (see especially chapters 5 and 13).

KEY POINTS

- Many people's self-image—the deeply held understanding of who they are at their core—is rooted in the views and expectations of family, mentors, and friends.
- A self-image based on approval or disapproval from others prevents personal growth. Self-images built on praise or admiration must be continually reinforced.
- Liberating your self-image from the external praise, criticism, and expectations of others will result in increased life satisfaction and well-being.
- Repeatedly evaluating the values that underlie your self-image serves as the core organizing principle of your actions.

CHAPTER THREE

OVERWHELMING OPPORTUNITIES

Freshman orientation was overwhelming for Laila and her new roommate, Carmen. The Club and Organization Fair, where student groups recruit incoming freshmen, was an especially daunting event. Dozens of overly enthusiastic upper-level students from dozens of clubs herded Carmen and Laila toward their booths and proclaimed the countless benefits of joining their organization through speeches, rapid-fire questions, and reams of pamphlets. They spoke with at least one hundred students before taking a break for lunch; they did not return to the fair that afternoon. A similar set of contrasting fears distressed both women. First, there were far more options than either could possibly consider, much less pursue. Both roommates were worried that they would regret choosing the "wrong" groups and miss out on "better" opportunities. Second, although many of the students they met appeared friendly and interesting, Laila and Carmen felt that their lack of experience and skill around the themes of each club made them unsuitable for membership. It was terrifying for them to think that they may be rejected by their peers during their first days on campus. Even worse, they were horrified at the prospect of embarrassing themselves in front of everyone if they participated in a club event. Despite experiencing similar fears, Laila and Carmen had different reactions, although neither chose a particularly productive path. Carmen's fear of missing out and fear of future regrets led her to try dozens of clubs and activities, lingering just long enough to put them on her résumé, but not long enough to actually experience the activities, to learn what she truly enjoyed, or to make any close friends. Laila's path, driven by her fear of embarrassment, led her to contact only three clubs, two of which she attended only the information session and never returned. Although she was a member of the surfing club for four years, she was already an excellent surfer and she knew many of the members from the surfing teams she had been on in high school. Neither of these paths allowed Laila or Carmen to learn new skills, explore their possibilities, or make lasting friends.

> *It is quality rather than quantity that matters.*
> —SENECA[1]

Every student's college experience is fundamentally different. Due to the staggering number of opportunities on every college campus, no student has the same set of adventures as any other student in history. Students are rarely even aware of all of the options since colleges rarely maintain a comprehensive list of all possible opportunities. Every year, people who have been on your campus for decades are still learning about multiple, long-established student opportunities (I heard about two opportunities for the first time in my fifteenth year of teaching, for example). The point is that there are many possibilities, but each student hears about a small fraction of them and participates in even fewer. Many students respond to the sheer number of choices in a similar way to Carmen and Laila.

Carmen's superficial participation in hundreds of activities was primarily driven by a fear of missing out (FOMO). As writer Etty Hillesum noted,[2] the "fear of missing out on things makes you miss out on everything." Many students today are aware of FOMO as the anxiety caused by social media posts that describe exciting events that may (or may not) be happening. The fear of missing critical opportunities, however, has a long history in human societies.[3] There has always been a fear that choosing one opportunity and missing another will put you at a disadvantage socially, academically, and professionally. The evidence suggests that some differences in access to opportunities can result in advantages on a broad scale, but it is unlikely that participating in extracurricular activities at college will result in any substantial advantages that are not available through other opportunities. By contrast, students who do not fully engage in any extracurricular activities, including some employment opportunities, suffer many substantive disadvantages.[4]

Many students become "résumé packers" or "badge collectors" out of a fear of missing out on opportunities. These students cycle through dozens of activities without making an impact or gaining any benefit. Despite the fact that these students boast about their long résumés—which can cause FOMO among their fellow students—no future employer, award selection committee, or admissions committee member has ever been fooled by these deceptive résumés. It is easy to recognize that these students have no deep or consequential experiences and are generally viewed negatively (see chapter 15). Equally important, these students never actually take advantage of the myriad opportunities during college, an important part of the college experience. Extracurricular activities serve a much more important purpose than gaining competitive advantages or building a long résumé. Students who bounce between opportunities do not learn what types of activities are satisfying and fulfilling to them, a foundation for choosing a fulfilling and satisfying career, nor do they form lifelong friendships despite thousands of acquaintances. Effort and dedication are required for any worthwhile endeavor; superficial efforts result in superficial results. That is, you reap what you sow.

Laila's choices were motivated largely by a fear of being embarrassed in front of her peers. For Laila, it is paramount that everyone thinks of her as a "success," similar to Marcus from chapter 2. The thought of failing—which, for many college students, includes not being "perfect"—challenges her self-image as a "success," which she desperately wants to maintain. As a result, Laila cannot try any new activity because she is very unlikely to be "the best" and will most likely be rather bad due to her lack of practice and experience. This fear drives her to stay within her comfort zone, participating only in activities and courses in which she already has some mastery. Though Laila may be superficially comfortable, she will miss out on the majority of the college experience available to her.[5] Importantly, she missed out on the main purpose of attending college: self-improvement and improved well-being. College is the ideal time to identify new interests, meet new people, and lay the foundation to flourish, none of which Laila will have the opportunity to do.

Laila, like so many of us, was not always so strongly influenced by her fear of embarrassment. While first learning to surf as a child, she was repeatedly tossed around by the waves. On more than one occasion she was afraid that she would drown, and she could not even stand on her board the first day. There was no doubt that she was not the best surfer on the water. Nevertheless, she enjoyed catching a few waves and was excited by her progress. Her enthusiasm increased as she progressed despite scrapes, bruises, and more near-drowning experiences through the years. As a child, she did not pay much attention to the judgments of her peers or coach. As a young woman, however, she has become acutely aware of both real and imagined judgments, leading her to avoid trying anything new for fear of embarrassment. Like most of us, you may have felt irrationally embarrassed by a poor performance, even if you had never attempted the activity before and thus had no reason to expect that you would perform well. Almost by definition, you will not be "good" at activities that you have never done before. Consequently, you might be hesitant to try something new for fear of embarrassment. Just imagine never experiencing anything new!

It is common for students to simultaneously feel both fear of missing opportunities and fear of embarrassment. These fears have varying effects on your decision-making and mental well-being over time and under different circumstances, but both are always present in novel situations. A delicate balance is essential to avoiding the extreme choices of trying as much as possible without obtaining any benefit and of trying only a few things in order to avoid embarrassment. In the exercises that follow, you will learn approaches to successfully explore your opportunities, identify appropriate activities to pursue, alleviate the fear of embarrassment that prevents you from pursuing opportunities, and feel satisfied with the pursuits you do choose without feeling that you missed out on others.

PRACTICE AND APPLICATION

Multiple practices will be introduced in this chapter to help you explore new activities without embarrassment and without regret about the activities you do not pursue. The specific situation may determine which approach is more effective than the others, which may change depending on the circumstances. Consider the approach that is most likely to help you in the situation you happen to be facing, even if it is not the approach with which you are most comfortable.

The Bigger Picture
College can be overwhelming. This is especially true when everything is new and coming at you at a head-spinning pace. There are so many possibilities on campus, how can you possibly explore them all? Put simply, you cannot. Although this response may initially cause anxiety, looking at the bigger picture can provide some inner calm. Each of us will experience only a minuscule fraction of the billions of possible activities that have been available to humans throughout history. It is clear from this perspective that trying *everything* is clearly impossible. Aiming to experience everything, or a large number of things, is destined for disappointment and failure. The more satisfying and fulfilling aim is to seek great experiences, regardless of the number of activities in which you participate. *Importantly, great experiences are not "great" because they are better than the experiences of your peers. A great experience is one that leads to well-being and life satisfaction, regardless of what others experience.* Participating in many different activities or trying to emulate the experiences of others will not make you happier or more fulfilled than engaging in a few activities that are meaningful to you. All evidence suggests that engaging in many different activities or trying to replicate the experiences of others will reduce your sense of well-being and life satisfaction.

Try the following each night this week to deal with your fear of missing out on important opportunities.

1. In a quiet place, set a timer for five minutes and close your eyes.
2. Bring your fear of missing a specific opportunity from the recent past or near future into your mind. This fear is often associated with opportunities that your peers may have that, if missed, could put you at some disadvantage.
3. Take a moment to visualize the details of the event or activity that is related to the fear of missing this specific opportunity.

4. Note your level of distress (0–100%) in your notebook.
5. Consider the disadvantages that missing this opportunity could cause, both big and small, against the disadvantages that you or others have experienced in the past when they missed opportunities. It is crucial to focus on the *actual* disadvantages that occurred because you did not participate in an event in which you had the opportunity to take part, rather than feelings about *potential* disadvantages. Examples of actual disadvantages could be missed networking connections that result in job offers to your peers or missing the only opportunity to learn an important skill. Potential disadvantages include thoughts like, *I might have missed meeting someone important* or *that could have turned out to be an important business opportunity*. Experiences that are useful for this practice focus on potential opportunities that you were anxious about missing and the *actual* negative consequences that resulted from missing those opportunities. Avoid focusing on opportunities that were never actually available to you, such as those you learn about after they happen, even if others benefited from them. It can also be useful to compare the disadvantages caused by missing your recent or upcoming opportunity to those who are in much worse situations, such as those living in war zones or during famines.
6. Note your level of distress about missing the opportunity again (0–100%) in your notebook.

This exercise will help you gain perspective on the true cost of missing one or even millions of opportunities. An elevated emotional state, such as fear, causes you to narrow your focus on a perceived problem, making it appear larger and more important than it really is.[6] Comparing your potential "missed opportunity" to past "missed opportunities" in your life or in the lives of others will reveal that your grandmother was in fact correct: "everything will turn out fine, it always does." You have been very successful despite missing thousands of opportunities, and you will continue to be successful despite missing many future opportunities. The greatest threat to your future success and current well-being is the *fear* of missing opportunities, not actually missing them. This exercise can also be applied to fear of embarrassment by substituting "the fear of embarrassment" in step 2 and "comparisons to supposedly embarrassing situations or events from your past" in step 4.

Fear of Missing Opportunities

Fear of missing opportunities is a classic example of misperception and mischaracterization. This type of fear causes people to feel regret before an event has even happened and to regret missing events that may never happen. Fear of missing opportunities is similar to the baby boomer phenomenon of "keeping up with the Joneses" and probably to many other cultural phenomena throughout history. These phenomena stem from the belief that experiences result in feelings of well-being or satisfaction only if they are *better* than the experiences of your peers. If the previous sentence sounds ridiculous, you have read it correctly.

In this approach, you will utilize wisdom from a *future* version of yourself. The first step in this exercise is to recall a time when you felt anxious about missing an event or opportunity, preferably one in which your peers later participated but you did not. Similar to the previous technique, choose an opportunity that you knew was going to occur before it actually occurred. Briefly describe the details of the opportunity in your notebook.

With the benefit of hindsight, write a brief description of the advantages your peers enjoyed *as a direct result* of participating in this event that you did not because you did not participate. These must be advantages that you never received, rather than ones you did receive but through alternative opportunities.

Now take a few minutes to explore, in writing, the importance of the missed advantages that you think could have been derived from this missed opportunity. That is, did the absence of these advantages hinder your progress or success in any way?

Similarly, take a few minutes to explore the negative impacts on your *well-being* that occurred because you were focused on missing the opportunity. That is, did you miss out on enjoying real moments in your life because you feared missing out on enjoyment elsewhere? In your notebook, compare the actual negative consequences of missing this opportunity with the suffering you experienced by focusing on the missed opportunity.

The task of identifying actual advantages that you did not receive as a result of missing out on an opportunity may have been quite challenging. The reason for this is that only a very small fraction of opportunities results in any tangible benefits, and most of the benefits are also available through other opportunities in which you may have taken part. Comparing what you lost by focusing on your fear with what others gained by participating was likely more apparent; you likely achieved similar success to your peers and thus did not "miss out" on the advantage, but you did suffer needlessly in the process.

In your notebook, write a short letter to yourself from "future you." This is equivalent to the earlier technique but instead of evaluating a past version of yourself, you will use the wisdom from a "future" version of yourself to help you with your current fear of missing out. "Future you" knows that your current fear of missing a specific opportunity harms your well-being and that the opportunity itself will likely not provide you with any substantial advantages that you cannot obtain elsewhere. This is similar to the way that "current you" knows (from the prior practice) that "past you" was only hurting yourself. Describe what "future you" would tell "current you" about the true value of the opportunity you are concerned about missing. What would "future you" think about the suffering you are currently causing yourself by worrying? What advice would "future you" give to "current you"?

Fear of Embarrassment

Fear of failing in front of others is a common barrier to trying new things. This fear, however, is also rooted in misperceptions. There is a common misconception that other people think about you and your actions all the time. They do not. People think primarily about themselves. Strangers and acquaintances may consider how you or your actions directly affect them, but they rarely do more than that. Most people will quickly forget about your lack of skills, especially if you enjoy yourself and are not bothered by it. Your friends, on the other hand, do think about you. But friends encourage well-intentioned ineptitude; they do not hold it against you. True friends encourage each other to try things that could improve well-being and life satisfaction and support each other in both success and failure. To be clear, I am not discussing obvious ethical failures (mean-spirited attacks, bigotry, etc.). In this case, I am discussing good-faith efforts in ethical activities for which you may not be highly skilled.

In your notebook, describe how the judgment of relative strangers *actually impacts* your life. That is, how does their negative view of your abilities affect you in a tangible way? Examples of tangible impacts could be the loss of friends, the loss of money, or even the strengthening of bonds between friends. Distinguish these tangible impacts that affect your future possibilities from those that only affect your *thoughts and emotions*. For example, emotions such as embarrassment may result from perceived negative thoughts, but they do not hinder your future directly.

You may notice that the opinions of relative strangers have little to no impact on anything other than your thoughts and emotions. It is possible for your thoughts and emotions to be profoundly affected by these opinions, but only if you allow them to do so. Whether the opinions of others affect your emotions and thoughts is something you can control (although it will take practice to limit the emotional impacts; see chapter 2). The objective of this approach is to help you internalize the accurate notion that others' opinions should not matter to you. Clearly describing the impact of putting your lack of experience on display will reduce or eliminate your fear of embarrassment, allowing you to try new things without fear.

PURSUIT OF THE GOOD LIFE

Now is the time to take advantage of the opportunities available to college students. If done well, you will discover the activities, employment opportunities, and future directions that will bring you life satisfaction and well-being. Taking part in these kinds of activities in college and throughout your life is crucial to your pursuit of the good life. The *fear of missing opportunities* causes many students to overextend themselves, briefly experimenting with many activities but gaining little from any one of them. The *fear of embarrassment*, on the other hand, prevents students from trying anything new. Although these responses are at opposite ends of the spectrum, the fears themselves are universal. In most novel situations, students simultaneously experience both fears to varying degrees. The purpose of this chapter is to help you reduce the impact of both of these fears on your life so that you can make the most of your college experiences. In chapter 4, we discuss how to balance these conflicting pressures in the specific arena of college social interactions.

KEY POINTS

- The thousands of extracurricular activities on most college campuses allow students to identify new interests, meet new people, and lay the foundation to flourish academically, professionally, and personally. However, many students fear that choosing inferior extracurriculars will put them at social, academic, or professional disadvantages.
- FOMO—the fear of missing opportunities—leads many students to bounce hastily between dozens of activities without gaining any benefit except padding their résumés; no employer, award selection committee, nor admissions committee member was ever fooled by these exaggerated résumés.
- Fear of embarrassment causes many students to participate only in activities in which they are already proficient, thus missing out on the true "college experience" and many opportunities for self-improvement and improved well-being.
- Reducing the impact of FOMO and the fear of embarrassment on your life will allow you to make the most of your college experience.

CHAPTER FOUR

CHOOSE FRIENDS PATIENTLY

Taylor was more than excited to embark on her college experience. She had thought that her college, which was two thousand miles from her family and high school friends, would provide a novel experience in a new environment with different weather, activities, and a new group of friends. Within a few weeks of arriving on campus, Taylor began feeling the effects of the geographical distance from her family and hometown friends, which deprived her of social support. Feelings of loneliness began to take root. Taylor met many students during freshman orientation, but she rarely felt comfortable at the many social functions organized by the college. Further, Taylor rarely interacted with her new roommates, as they already had a close group of friends they had made during summer workouts for the school's soccer team. So when a sophomore in her dorm invited Taylor to join their fraternity, she was relieved. The fraternity members were nice and dedicated to the mission of the fraternity, which focused mainly on politics. Taylor felt this was her opportunity to build lifelong friendships like those she observed among her parents' college friends. This did not progress the way that Taylor had hoped. Taylor had never been interested in politics and struggled to understand what motivated her new fraternity brothers and sisters. Taylor found herself pretending to be interested in politics, spending most of her free time on fraternity-organized activities, and even began dressing and speaking like others in the fraternity. Despite her efforts, Taylor never made genuine connections with any of her fraternity brothers or sisters. Her time spent on fraternity-related activities also prevented her from meeting other people with closer interests and values and with whom she could have formed genuine connections. Even though Taylor spoke, dressed, and acted like others in the fraternity, she never felt fully integrated. The feelings of loneliness Taylor experienced during freshman orientation continued throughout her college experience.

> *If you choose bad companions, no one will believe that you are anything but bad yourself.*
> —AESOP'S FABLES[1]

Loneliness is distressing in the moment but rarely catastrophic if experienced in a limited time frame. To be clear, prolonged loneliness can affect your physical and mental health and should be addressed in consultation with a mental health professional. Transient feelings of loneliness, such as those you might experience during your first semester at college, are almost universal. In fact, every individual experiences feelings of loneliness at some point in their lives, especially when their social networks are disrupted, such as when they move away from friends and family to attend college.[2] Temporary loneliness is a common experience, and the regularity with which nearly everyone overcomes it suggests that you, too, will be able to overcome the feelings of loneliness whenever they arise.

Feelings of loneliness arise when people sense an absence of genuine connections with the people with whom they regularly interact.[3] Loneliness, however, is not the same as being alone. Nearly every student feels lonely when starting college despite living in close quarters with other students and attending many new-student social events, classes, and parties filled with their peers. Nevertheless, these temporary feelings of loneliness often motivate new students to spend excessive energy trying to quickly make friends. These students incorrectly believe that any acquaintance can relieve their loneliness; they do not.[4] Often, these fast-forming acquaintanceships occur between students who hold incompatible values, which undermines the formation of genuine connections and rarely eliminates (and can intensify) feelings of loneliness. Genuine social connections that alleviate loneliness can only develop over time with people who share and support your core values (see chapter 2).

Taylor bypassed a slow but effective solution—genuine friendships—in favor of a quick but flawed solution—superficial connections—in an attempt to ease the discomfort of loneliness as quickly as possible. Students using Taylor's strategy make many acquaintances, none of whom can alleviate their feelings of loneliness.[5] As the first president of the United States of America advised, "It is better to be alone than in bad company."[6] Furthermore, the time and effort required to maintain these loosely held acquaintances is time that can no longer be used to form and maintain real friendships.

Why do so many students, like Taylor, join the first group they can find when it rarely provides the benefit they seek? The evolution of sociality among humans and other primates provides several answers. As an example, social bonds were essential for survival and reproduction in prehistoric human societies as well as within other primate groups.[7] Without a social group, individuals were less likely to find and defend food sources, less likely to mate and reproduce, and more vulnerable to attacks by other individuals. Social groups that are strong and dependable insulate their members from both the threat and the reality of physical harm, a phenomenon that can still be observed in schoolyards and on television. Importantly, the dependability of a social group, or the likelihood of group members aiding each other, is strongly contingent on the strength of social bonds within the group. As a result, it appears that the motivation to eliminate feelings of loneliness quickly by seeking social connections is an evolved trait in humans.[8] Even though social groups are no longer necessary for survival and reproduction, modern humans have maintained the instinct to join social groups. Similarly, we have maintained the instinct to avoid *appearing* as if we were not a member of a social group, which would make us an easy target, even though social groups are rarely needed for physical protection in modern society. Thus, our motivation to join a group at the earliest opportunity is both driven by a desire to alleviate loneliness through social bonding as well as an external desire to avoid the appearance of being alone.

Although assimilating into the first available group can reduce the discomfort associated with the appearance of being alone, it cannot alleviate the feelings of loneliness.[9] Further, assimilating into groups that do not share your values can be destructive to your personal growth and your future. Exaggerated examples can be found in young adult movies that depict a "good kid" who gets involved with a tough crowd (imagine leather jackets and greased hair), participates in dangerous activities (smoking cigarettes and driving fast cars), and compromises his or her once-promising future. Even if you are unlikely to join the Sharks or the Jets from *West Side Story*, participating in activities that do not foster self-improvement in ways consistent with your values will still hinder your progress toward your goals. Further, assimilation into a group with different values can result in acting, speaking, and behaving in ways that are incompatible with your core beliefs. The disconnect between your behaviors and your values (see chapter 2) will cause anxiety and increased feelings of loneliness. Furthermore, you will miss opportunities to connect with others who share your values and aspirations.

A careful, patient, and rational evaluation of the values of potential friends is vital to your well-being, life satisfaction, and the person you will become. An individual's social connections influence a variety of aspects of their lives, including their goals, behaviors, emotions, and values.[10] For example, you have likely noticed that members of social groups tend to make similar fashion choices, have similar goals, and are often of a similar frame of mind. Group members' choices and emotional states are contagious and spread rapidly to other members. Ideally, your college friends will promote your well-being and aid your self-improvement in ways that align with your values. Although you should not necessarily rank others by their potential to improve your life, choosing friendships that support your core values and enhance your well-being is far superior to choosing destructive relationships or numerous acquaintances that have little positive impact on your life. As ancient wisdom recommends, "The key is to keep company only with people who uplift you, whose presence calls forth your best."[11] Identifying and pursuing friendships based on shared values provides the foundation for developing genuine connections.

In light of the advantages of quality friendships and the disadvantages of relationships that hinder personal growth, why do so many students choose suboptimal social groups? Three notable reasons suggest that (a) students rarely define their values and ambitions (see chapter 2) and therefore fail to recognize traits that are important in potential friends; (b) students may fear they are not good enough for, and will be rejected by, those whose character they admire (as discussed in chapter 3); and (c) there is a tendency among students to pursue acquaintances who will assist them in their academic or career success but who will not develop into lasting friendships. The last motivation, pursuing functional acquaintances to help academic success, has become more common as our society becomes more competitive. It is common for students to focus on metrics of "success" and view social interactions as tools for their own advancement. These types of relationships are not friendships, but rather transactions akin to business partnerships. I will not argue against pursuing connections that will benefit your academic career, but I will argue against exclusively developing such relationships. You cannot replace genuine personal connections with connections made for the express purpose of assisting your studies.

PRACTICE AND APPLICATION

Acknowledge the Source of Loneliness

The first step in choosing optimal friendships is to recognize and acknowledge the causes and consequences of your feelings of loneliness. Loneliness is associated with the innate desire in humans to form social groups that, for our ancestors, provided protection and food. In modern societies, however, this instinct is not always helpful and can be detrimental, similar to other vestigial structures such as wisdom teeth or the appendix. The absence of a stable friend group for a limited time is not physically damaging and is far preferable to spending time pursuing unproductive or destructive relationships. By acknowledging the sources of your loneliness, you can put it into perspective and make more rational and beneficial choices. That is, the feelings associated with limited periods of loneliness are not actually painful, they are just a set of very uncomfortable thoughts that should not guide your decisions.

To begin, sit for three minutes with your eyes closed and concentrate on what loneliness "feels" like. Address the following questions in your notebook: Where in your body do you feel the loneliness? What are the bodily sensations associated with loneliness? Are those bodily sensations painful, or do you just associate them with negative feelings?

You might notice that there are physical sensations connected to loneliness, but none of them is physically painful. The negative thoughts associated with these bodily sensations can be emotionally painful, but the sensations themselves are not physically painful. You might also find that taking the time to reflect on how loneliness feels can make loneliness less frightening and ease the emotional sting of the feelings when they do occur. In the event that these feelings are physically painful or if your anxiety about loneliness increased after this exercise, please seek assistance from a mental health professional.

In your notebook, describe how the absence of a supportive social group directly impacts your life. Take care to distinguish irrefutable impacts on your goals, values, or capacity for self-improvement from outcomes that may or may not occur. For example, you may believe that other students judge you, but it is unlikely that you know this to be true (it is also unlikely to be true; most people think almost exclusively about themselves).

It is likely that you had difficulty identifying any concrete consequences caused by a short-term absence of a supportive social group. This is because short periods without a social group generally have few direct negative effects on your life, except that you instinctively assume it to be negative. That is, the negative aspects of not having a friend group derive primarily from how humans have evolved to think about not having a friend group. The purpose of this exercise is to empower you to challenge these instinctual thoughts, which will give you the ability to make rational decisions when seeking quality relationships.[12] This is not meant to suggest that you should not pursue a supportive social group (you should) or that having quality friends will not positively impact your life (they will). However, the benefits of being part of a social group are only realized when you establish friendships with people who have compatible values and allow those friendships to develop.

Clarify the Values You Want in Your Friends

People are complex and attempting to define them will rarely help you or them (see chapter 2). Authentic friendships, however, are built on identifying characteristics and values that you admire in another person. Establishing the values and characteristics that you hold in high regard is essential to building quality relationships. Although nobody is perfect, having friends with compatible values provides a foundation for a fulfilling college experience and supports your pursuit of the good life. Remember that you are not searching for *the* best people, you are searching for the best people for you. By describing the traits you value in a friend in writing, you will force yourself to contemplate previously subconscious and potentially contradictory ideas. Furthermore, you may recognize toxic traits you are drawn to but know you should avoid. In your notebook, describe characteristics, values, ambitions, and behaviors that you admire and would welcome in a friend. A good place to start is by remembering traits of past friends and family members you admire and that have contributed to your personal growth and well-being.

This list will help you identify peers with whom you can form genuine connections. It is likely that you will be a better, happier, and more satisfied person if you have friends who share the values you have identified. These friends will influence your behaviors in ways that align with your goals and values, support you in good times and bad, and can facilitate your academic and career success. Psychological research has found that friends emulate one another, so that beneficial decisions arise from interactions with admirable people.[13] You will be able to live according to your values if you surround yourself with people whose values you admire. Continue to revisit this exercise throughout your life as you gain a deeper understanding of yourself and as your values change over time. In addition to reminding yourself of your own values, this exercise can ensure that these values drive your decisions.

Pursuing Friendships

Pursuing new friendships can be scary. What if you are rejected by the quality people whose values and judgments you admire and respect? Does this indicate that you lack the character traits that quality people admire and respect? It does not. Intriguingly, it does not have a consistent meaning. You might not develop a lasting friendship with someone you respect for a variety of reasons, most of which have nothing to do with you. Inopportune timing, a full social calendar, shyness, and fear all impact the choices of your peers (nobody is perfect), none of which is within your control. Nevertheless, the fear of rejection can prevent you from pursuing quality friendships and lead you to settle for loosely held acquaintances where the fear of rejection is absent.

The bodily sensations associated with rejection, like the sensations associated with loneliness, are not physically painful. Instead, they are associated with anxiety about how others might perceive you and about your own perception of yourself (see chapter 2). In your notebook, describe what rejection—or your fear of rejection—actually feels like. In other words, where in your body do you feel the fear of rejection? What are the sensations associated with rejection? Are those sensations painful, or do they simply have a negative connotation for you?

It is likely that you can recognize that these feelings are not physically painful, similar to the first exercise. These sensations are associated with anxiety and challenges to your self-image, which can be emotionally painful, but they are not physically painful on their own. Also similar to the first exercise, you might find that taking the time to examine what rejection actually feels like can make it less frightening and easier to deal with when it does happen.

Describe what underlies your fear of rejection in your notebook. That is, are there any negative outcomes you expect to actually occur if you do not succeed in befriending a peer? Do any of these negative outcomes have a high probability of occurring? Be careful to distinguish irrefutable impacts on your goals, values, or self-improvement from disputable impacts that may only happen in your thoughts.

You can recognize the actual impact of social rejection by contextualizing your fears. For example, many of us have felt the temporary pain of rejection, which had only a small impact on our lives. Write a brief description of an event in which you felt rejected in your notebook.

Now take a few minutes with your notebook to explore the long-lasting negative impacts on your life that occurred as a result of this rejection. That is, do you think your life now is worse than it would have been if you had not been rejected?

Lasting negative impacts on your life were probably quite difficult to identify. This is because rejection is common but rarely has any lasting negative effects. In fact, chances are that you never even think about times when you were rejected. You may even feel lucky that you were rejected, that your life would have been much worse if you had not been rejected (I have had many, many such experiences). This perspective allows you to appreciate that any future rejection will also have a negligible effect on your life. Conversely, not pursuing quality relationships due to fear of rejection will have the extremely negative impact of preventing genuine relationships from developing.

In your notebook, write a short letter to yourself from "future you," similar to the approach introduced in chapter 3. In this case, you will use the wisdom of a future version of yourself who understands that rejection will not have any lasting impacts on your life. "Future you" also knows the negative consequences of not cultivating quality friendships (no quality friends). Imagine what "future you" would think about your current fear of rejection. What advice would "future you" give to current you?

As you gain a better understanding of the impacts of rejection along with the benefits of building genuine friendships, consider how to overcome your fear of rejection when pursuing a quality friendship. While it is unlikely that any approach will completely eliminate your fear of rejection, creating a plan to recognize and limit the influence of fearful thoughts will allow you to make favorable decisions. In your notebook, briefly describe the thoughts or sensations that you associate with fear of rejection. That is, describe what you feel in your body and mind when you consider approaching someone you want to befriend. Additionally, write a statement that challenges the validity of each thought or sensation. For example, *I fear that the other person will view me as desperate and mock me to their friends. I can challenge this idea by pointing out that it is extremely unlikely that anyone would do this (unless they are playing a role in a movie). Additionally, any person who would do such a thing does not share my values and thus could not become a genuine friend anyway.*

PURSUIT OF THE GOOD LIFE

There are many people who maintain meaningful relationships with their college friends throughout their lives. These types of genuine friendships are integral to overall life satisfaction, well-being, and the pursuit of the good life. Genuine friendships are also conducive to self-discovery, self-improvement, and strengthening your values during college. However, these benefits can be derived only from genuine friendships based on compatible values. Taking the time to discover and build authentic friendships in college will be one of the most beneficial things you can do, despite short-term discomfort associated with feelings of loneliness. Your social group will be a reliable support system in good times and in bad, helping you to maintain your peace of mind regardless of the circumstances. Your social group is vital in your pursuit of the good life. Although this chapter recommends evaluating the character and values of others as a basis for forming lasting friendships, it should not be used to "rank" or feel superior to others. Though people with values and aspirations that do not complement your own may not be the ideal friends for you, that does not mean they have poor character or values. The purpose of assessing the values and traits of others should be only to identify individuals with whom you can build meaningful relationships. An important caveat to the lessons in this chapter is that, unlike temporary loneliness, extended periods of loneliness can be detrimental to your mental and physical health and should be addressed with the help of a mental health professional.

KEY POINTS

- Nearly every person experiences loneliness when their social networks are disrupted, like attending college far from friends and family. Transient feelings of loneliness arise in the absence of genuine connections within your immediate social circle.
- Modern humans have maintained an evolved instinct to quickly eliminate feelings of loneliness.
- Assimilating into a social group that does not share your values is destructive to your well-being as the disconnect between your behaviors and values causes anxiety and can increase feelings of loneliness.
- Genuine social connections that alleviate loneliness and enhance your well-being develop over time with people who share and support your core values.

CHAPTER FIVE

INTRINSIC MOTIVATION

Luca was always able to find motivation for school and extracurricular activities before starting college. His motivation for each activity was always clear: Winning praise and prizes for his athletic ability kept him motivated in sports while fear of punishment or criticism from his parents, teachers, and peers motivated his studies. His parents also kept him on schedule, reminding or pressuring him to practice or study. There was never a moment that Luca did not know what he should be doing nor what motivated him into action. Now that Luca is halfway through his first semester of college, he is having difficulty finding motivation to study. There are so few exams in college courses that Luca cannot rely on them as a source of motivation. In addition, neither his professors nor peers seem to care how well he performs on his exams. As an example, neither his professors nor peers praised him for his performance on the first calculus midterm, nor did they mention his poor mark on the French midterm. The absence of awards, admiration, and admonishment suggests to him that no one cares about his course performance in the ways that motivated him during high school. That no one in college is concerned with his performance on exams was further supported when both his calculus and French professors lectured him for using office hours to discuss his grade and not course material. Although Luca is interested in the course material, he finds studying to be strenuous and stressful. It is just not clear to Luca why studying is worth the effort and stress when he could spend his time with his friends, at his part-time job, or at some of the hundreds of fun college activities. Although the importance of sports and his studies was so obvious when he was in high school, Luca simply cannot remember why he had ever thought it was important to spend his weekends studying as opposed to having fun with his friends.

> *You have power over your mind—not outside events.*
> *Realise this, and you will find strength.*
> —MARCUS AURELIUS ANTONINUS[1]

Motivation can be hard to find and even harder to sustain. Many people are motivated by the possibility of illustrious success in the form of money, awards, recognition, and power (see chapter 2). It is not surprising that these externally driven metrics of success motivate people. The entertainment media and our own experiences suggest that our place within social hierarchies is a function of respect that is determined, at least in part, by the accumulation of accolades, money, and power.

Humans are social creatures that have an innate drive to ascend social hierarchies that, among our ancestors, determined who had access to food and mates. In modern societies, however, accumulating money or accolades rarely results in life satisfaction.[2] Ironically, people motivated exclusively by money, praise, or respect often fail to attain them. Even more paradoxically, those that do accumulate great wealth or high praise are often unhappy and almost never satisfied.[3] A primary reason that people focused on external metrics of success often fail to achieve those successes is that the outcomes—accumulating money or praise—are not in their complete control. The Serenity Prayer by Reinhold Niebuhr counsels, "God, grant me the serenity to accept the things I cannot change, courage to change the things I can, and wisdom to know the difference."[4] The lack of control over your goals can result in frustration, insecurity, and apathy, all of which rapidly erode motivation.

Academic, career, material, and interpersonal success are all *external* motivators, also called extrinsic motivation.[5] Extrinsic motivation is driven by the desire to obtain rewards and avoid punishments from others in society. Although you can influence the probability of attaining an extrinsic goal, the ultimate outcome is not within your complete control. The actions of other people as well as random chance—neither of which you control—at least partially determine if you will receive recognition or avoid criticism. As an example, intensive training will increase the probability of winning a race, but actually winning depends upon several factors beyond your control, including the conditions of the track, how well you slept, and the speed of your competitors. You may train sufficiently to break the track record and still lose to an even faster racer. Similarly, studying will improve the probability that you score well on an exam, but you cannot control which questions are asked, how the professor grades your answers, nor if another student who barely studied scores as well as you by pure luck. You can influence your chances of attaining extrinsic goals but actually attaining these goals is not within your complete control.

Extrinsic motivators like financial wealth or glowing exam scores externalize the *locus of control* such that you do not feel in command of your life.[6] Feeling as if you are not in control erodes motivation due to the disconnect between your efforts to achieve your goal and actually achieving your goal. This disconnect can make you question if your effort is, well, worth the effort. For example, if all your thoughts and actions are focused on improving your exam score, your motivation to study will slowly crumble due to the disconnect between your effort to learn the material—which is in your complete control—and the exam score you receive—which you can influence but do not actually control.

The focus on exam results also amplifies your anxiety about failing to achieve your desired score, which will further diminish your motivation.[7] This anxiety often causes students to internalize the false belief that *trying* and doing poorly on an exam is more detrimental to your self-image and reputation than *not trying* and doing poorly (see chapter 2).[8] In reality, "You never fail until you stop trying."[9] It may be impossible to completely disregard extrinsic goals, but it is possible to accept that many things are beyond your control. Although accepting "the things I cannot change" may seem defeatist and scary at first, it does not have to be. There is a liberating alternative mindset that guarantees perpetual success: *intrinsic motivation*.

Intrinsic motivation refers to actions that are driven only by your internal objectives (well-being and satisfaction) and are completely controlled by you.[10] Goals that are intrinsically motivated are things you desire regardless of their potential to yield recognition, money, good grades, or other extrinsic benefits. As an example, the desire to watch a nature documentary about sharks is inherently enjoyable for me (intrinsic motivation), not because I will win a trophy for my impressive shark knowledge (extrinsic motivation). Intrinsically motivated goals are generally under your complete control and are often progress oriented rather than outcome oriented.[11] That is, learning about sharks is in my complete control—there is plenty to read and watch—and learning itself is a journey that does not have an "outcome"—there is always something more to learn. I can never fail to achieve my intrinsically motivated goal to learn more about sharks and I will always enjoy my time while constantly achieving this goal.

It may not be obvious that all of your behaviors and actions can be exclusively intrinsically motivated. After all, your decisions are also influenced by external factors such as family obligations, jobs, and classes. However, even these seemingly external factors can be motivated by internal objectives. For example, the obligation to study for your exams could be motivated by fear of failing your courses (extrinsic) or, hopefully, by your genuine desire for self-improvement through learning the course material (intrinsic). Intrinsic motivators are inherently satisfying and enjoyable and thus cannot diminish your motivation (see table that follows). Importantly, you will always achieve your intrinsic, progress-oriented goals and there will never be a motivation-eroding disconnect between your actions and the goal itself (see figure in chapter 11).

Intrinsically motivated people experience greater well-being, are more satisfied, and paradoxically, are even more likely to achieve external success.[12] That is, students who focus on learning the material achieve higher exam scores than students who focus on earning high exam scores.[13] Students who focus exclusively on learning the material are also less anxious and enjoy their time studying.[14] It may now seem obvious why internal motivation results in life satisfaction: it is better to enjoy what you are doing while achieving your intrinsic goal than to be anxious while trying to achieve your external goal whose outcome is often disappointing. If you are going to do it anyway, you might as well enjoy it.

EXTRINSICALLY MOTIVATED	INTRINSICALLY MOTIVATED
Studying to achieve good grades to impress your professors, peers, or parents.	Studying because you enjoy learning the material.
Joining a study group in order to show off your ostentatious erudition.	Participating in a study group to better learn the course material by contemplating the views of others and through teaching your peers.
Taking your grandmother to her medical appointments to avoid nagging or punishment.	Caring for your grandmother because you desire to improve the well-being of your family.
Socializing with someone because they can further your social standing or your career.	Socializing with someone because you enjoy their company.
Volunteering because it looks good on medical school applications.	Volunteering because it increases your well-being and life satisfaction.

When it comes to studying, what could be more motivating than wanting to learn the material while enjoying doing so? It may be necessary to reframe your current extrinsic goals centered on exam scores into intrinsic goals centered on your own well-being and satisfaction. It is essential to think about why you want what you want in order to reframe your goals. For example, you are likely to be disappointed if you are motivated to study in order to impress your professors or classmates (extrinsic motivation). You may learn the material, at least temporarily, but studying will be burdensome. Moreover, when your professors and classmates are not impressed, your motivation will quickly fade and you will be less likely to study for future exams. In other words, failing to achieve your extrinsic goals—in this case impressing your professors and peers—will rapidly diminish your motivation. Reframing this extrinsic motivation into a progress-oriented, internally satisfying goal can result only in satisfaction, well-being, and continued motivation to continue enjoying the process of learning. As an important side note, there is a difference between what you *feel* like doing and what you *want* to do. Studying takes effort and you may not *feel* like doing it at times, even if you truly enjoy learning the material. In spite of this, enjoying the learning process is the best way to keep motivation high.

Many religions, philosophies, and schools of psychology acknowledge that much of human suffering is caused by the disconnect between the outcome you desire and what actually occurs.[15] Thus, suffering arises from wanting what you cannot control.[16] The desire for wealth, recognition, or other things beyond your control will inevitably lead to a decline in your well-being, since you will regularly fail to achieve what you cannot control. For example, I would like to win millions in the lottery, but I cannot control which numbers are chosen, resulting in disappointment after disappointment. If you reframe your goals, you will stop yearning for things that are beyond your control and desire only what you are guaranteed to achieve.

You may be reluctant to abandon your current focus on grades and material success. After all, you have been successful thus far by focusing on extrinsic goals. Although it can be unnerving, refocusing on intrinsic goals has many benefits. Several studies have shown that people who believe they control the outcomes of their endeavors are happier and are also more successful at acquiring material success and recognition.[17] Conversely, people who believe their success depends on external factors are miserable and give up easily. Most importantly, you will always achieve your intrinsically motivated goals if you desire only what is in your complete control. Frustration and anxiety in your life can be greatly eased if you are certain you can reach your goals.

It might seem surprising that focusing on intrinsic goals leads to more extrinsic success than focusing on achieving extrinsic success. However, intrinsically motivated people are focused on the processes needed to achieve success and are less consumed with anxiety about the outcome.[18] For example, dedicating all your mental energy to learning the material is more likely to result in a good exam score than spending part of your mental energy worrying about what a bad mark might mean for your course grade (or how your father will react, or if you will have to take summer school, or if you will ever get into law school, et cetera).

PRACTICE AND APPLICATION

The exercises in this chapter provide an approach to identify your intrinsic motivation. Despite the examples focusing on exams and studying, this approach can be applied to any activity for which you are typically unmotivated or that has previously been motivated by external objectives. Identifying your intrinsic motivation in college will lessen your anxiety and propel you in your pursuit of the good life in college. I recommend first practicing the following exercises by focusing on a course in which you have a quiz or exam. In your notebook, describe how you would define "success" for this upcoming exam or quiz.

Now write a description of the thoughts and feelings that came to mind when you were thinking about the exam and your definition of success. Did you think about the grade you might get, a looming sense of disappointment, nervous excitement at the thought of a good score, resistance, tiredness at the thought of how much you will need to study, or any other feelings about the outcome of the exam? What effect do thoughts about your potential exam result have on your mental well-being?

Now describe the benefits of achieving the success you described. Include how you think achieving this success will make you feel and how long you will feel this way. Your experience with previous exams can help you distinguish between the benefits you actually receive from achieving your desired outcome and expected benefits that rarely materialize.

Similarly, write how failing to achieve the success as you defined it would negatively affect your life. Concentrate on outcomes that have a high probability of occurring, not those that you fear will happen but probably will not. How would not achieving this success, and experiencing the associated negative effects, make you feel and for how long?

Replacing the extrinsic motivations you have written above with intrinsic motivators will take practice, but it is worth the effort. As an example, imagine participating in a competitive event such as tennis or chess. Replacing the extrinsic goal of winning your match with an intrinsic goal like improving your technical skills, building social connections, or having fun will eliminate anxiety you may have about the match.

In your notebook, describe at least one intrinsic motivation for your upcoming exam. Make sure this intrinsic goal is within your control and is progress oriented rather than outcome oriented. As a reminder, "I genuinely enjoy learning about sharks" is an intrinsically motivated, progress-oriented goal that is completely within your control, whereas "Learning about sharks will improve my exam score" is an extrinsically motivated, outcome-oriented goal that is *not* within your complete control.

Please write a definition for how you would define "success" for these intrinsic goals. That is, how is achieving this goal inherently rewarding, satisfying, or stress reducing?

Focusing on the benefits of intrinsic goals is an important step in reframing your motivation. First, assess whether your intrinsic goal is likely to be achieved. Next, determine if you are more likely to achieve your *external* goal if you are intrinsically or extrinsically motivated. For example, decide whether you are more likely to perform well on your exam if you focus exclusively on learning the material (intrinsic) or if you think about the score you might receive and what that means about you or your future. Please write at least one additional reason why intrinsic motivation is more likely to lead to a better score than extrinsic motivation.

Most students define success as "doing well on their exams," as you may have done to begin these exercises. This definition of success almost always leads to anxiety, which will reduce your motivation to study and, paradoxically, will reduce your chance of achieving "success" according to your original definition. Even when students do well, they often feel nothing more positive than *relief*, and even this *blah* feeling generally lasts only a short time. Focusing on learning and self-improvement, on the other hand, always results in optimism and well-being. These vibrant feelings arise from knowing that you are highly likely to achieve your intrinsically motivated goal. Collectively, intrinsically motivated goals increase motivation, decrease stress, and increase your chance of performing well, all while enjoying yourself. In your pursuit of the good life in college, intrinsic motivation is essential.

PURSUIT OF THE GOOD LIFE

This chapter describes how to reframe your current desires and goals to reduce anxiety, increase your life satisfaction, and pursue the good life during college. The approaches described promote a focus on intrinsically motivated goals that are progress oriented and within your complete control. The intrinsic motivation you feel will never diminish because you will always achieve your objectives (you are in control of the outcome) and the process of achieving your objectives is inherently satisfying and often enjoyable. Ironically, focusing your energy on pursuing intrinsic goals will also make external success more likely, although you may not care if you have completely refocused on intrinsically motivated goals. For example, a person who wants to improve their personal health has an easier time motivating themselves to exercise than someone who wants others to see them as more attractive; the proximate goal is the same—a healthier body—but the ultimate goal, motivation, and likelihood of success are quite different.

KEY POINTS

- People who are primarily concerned with external metrics of success—like accumulating wealth or praise—are often unhappy because achieving these goals is not in their complete control.
- The absence of control causes frustration, insecurity, and apathy, reducing motivation due to the disconnect between your efforts and your achievements.
- Extrinsic motivators are societal rewards and punishments; you can influence your chances of attaining extrinsic goals but you cannot control the outcomes.
- Intrinsic motivators are internal (well-being and satisfaction), are completely within your control, and are often progress oriented rather than outcome oriented. Intrinsic motivators are inherently satisfying and do not diminish motivation.
- Intrinsically motivated people experience greater well-being, are more satisfied, and, paradoxically, are more likely to achieve external success.

CHAPTER SIX

BUSYNESS IS NOT PRODUCTIVE

Ann Marie was constantly busy in high school. Her life consisted of school, homework, softball practice, piano lessons, and her part-time job, totaling fourteen hours a day; every waking moment of her life was scheduled. There were, however, few activities that required a great deal of concentration or effort. By contrast, the majority of Ann Marie's time in college is unscheduled. She is required to be somewhere only during the scheduled hours at her on-campus job, twelve hours per week, and during class time, about eight hours a week, and many of her classmates do not even go to class!

The difference between her hectic high school schedule and the near absence of scheduled time in college has caused Ann Marie a few conflicting problems. First, her college classes have only a handful of major exams or projects, with very little graded work in between, unlike the constant flow of mundane worksheets in high school. Several professors stated on the first day of class that college courses are challenging and will require dedicated mental focus for five to ten hours outside of class each week so as to not fall behind. Ann Marie recognizes the importance of maintaining a regular study schedule after her poor performance on her first exam. However, she has no one to enforce a schedule or ensure that she uses her time efficiently. Second, Ann Marie is uncomfortable with her unscheduled time. The fact that everyone else claims to be so busy makes her worry that she must be missing out on valuable opportunities. She worries that she is not making the most of her time. She worries that her peers and professors will think she is not important enough to participate in valuable activities. She filled her free time by joining multiple groups and clubs to combat these concerns, but most of them only moderately interest her and none can help her achieve her goals or improve her quality of life. So she scrolls social media during her commute and in the evenings to fill the time with some activity. Although these activities relieved her anxiety related to idleness, her schedule now is so hectic that she barely has time to study.

> *It is essential for you to remember that the attention you give to any action should be in due proportion to its worth, for then you won't tire and give up, if you aren't busying yourself with lesser things beyond what should be allowed.*
> —MARCUS AURELIUS ANTONINUS[1]

It has become a badge of pride in our fast-paced culture to be busy. Our increasingly connected world has made "being busy" itself a commodity with apparent value, as opposed to prioritizing progress toward our goals and well-being. The concept of busyness has become a substitute for importance, a symbol of our value in society, and a way for people to demonstrate that they have a full and engaging life.[2] As a society, we often associate constant activity with responsible, productive, and worthy people, whereas calmness and tranquility are often associated with laziness and selfishness.[3] When people say, "I am sooo busy," they are trying to imply, "I am important" and "I am valuable." The assumption that busyness equates to a person's value is prevalent but dangerously illogical.

The relationship between busyness and social prominence is readily apparent in modern societies. The lead character in most young adult movies expresses anxiety about not being invited to the big high school social event, not because they want to participate, but because our society equates social plans with social status. Although the rational basis of this association is questionable in the real world, the educational counterpart is completely absurd. Completing coursework so that you can better financially support yourself or engage in leisure activities that promote your life satisfaction is a much more rational indication of your capacity as a student, although the benefit of *demonstrating your capacity as a student* is unclear. Professors care only that you learn the material, not how quickly you learn the material or how busy you are in general.

The feelings of discomfort associated with inactivity and calmness are as strong as the desire for activity.[4] An idle mind can fill itself with anxiety-inducing what-ifs about past events or projections about a miserable future, neither of which helps in planning or improving well-being.[5] The thoughts of an idle mind tend to be circular, running and rerunning scenarios that have only questionable connections to reality.[6] These circular thoughts can spiral into worst-case scenarios that feel impossible to escape. As an example, a fleeting thought about an upcoming quiz can transform into a growing flood of concerns about the course, graduation, and your career (you will see this in Arjun's story in chapter 8). Being alone with these troubling thoughts can be intolerable, causing us to feel fidgety and desperate for a distraction to numb the pain. The relief from anxiety provided by distractions, such as scrolling through social media or reading the news, is minimal and provides only temporary relief. The act of engaging with your thoughts, albeit temporarily uncomfortable, results in long-term tranquility and improved well-being.[7] Engaging with troubling thoughts can be best accomplished with the help of a therapist for some people.

Many students have obligations beyond their control, such as jobs needed to ease financial hardships or family obligations, which add substantially to their total scheduled time and to actual busyness. Obligations beyond your control are part of your scheduled time, like coursework, and though they increase your actual busyness, they are necessary for your productivity and your well-being. Nevertheless, many students with and without extensive obligatory time commitments overschedule their unscheduled free time to appear even busier, resulting in stress and reduced productivity.

Whatever the reason for overscheduling yourself, the end result is the same: activity without purpose. Ironically, people often cite busyness as an excuse to neglect responsibilities and to abandon their core principles. That is, people use "busyness" to justify not listening, dishonesty, tardiness, being inconsiderate, and, unexpectedly, for being unproductive.[8] Busyness even serves as an excuse to avoid engaging in productive and valuable activities. Many "busy" people believe that their busyness makes them appear important; however, busyness actually prevents them from doing important things and from actually being important. The reason is that people focused on busyness are rarely effective, whereas people focused on productivity are effective because they concentrate on important things.

Productivity is much more than checking items off your to-do list. In fact, completing tasks is only productive as a means of self-improvement, which is an essential part of living a fulfilling and meaningful life. Productive activities are those that expand your core values (self-improvement, justice, courage, and interpersonal connections; see the appendix to this book). Your productivity to-do list should also include actions that promote well-being—an integral part of self-improvement—such as self-care, leisure, and social connections. Take care to ensure that these activities do, in fact, contribute to your well-being and are not just mild distractions that keep you busy and divert your mind from stressful

BUSY PEOPLE...	PRODUCTIVE PEOPLE...
try to impress others with their activities.	focus on their own well-being and life satisfaction.
work toward the appearance of a life mission.	have a well-thought-out and clearly defined mission.
multitask.	focus on one task at a time.
have many constantly changing priorities.	have a few well-thought-through priorities.
focus on action.	focus on designing careful plans to achieve high-value goals.
talk about how busy they are.	make time for important tasks.
work toward unimportant goals.	prioritize and work toward important goals.
equate action with accomplishment.	carefully determine a path to achieve goals with the least cost in time and resources.

thoughts. You can distinguish between distractions and productive activities by determining if you feel just as stressed after completing an activity as you did before (distraction) or are more energized after completing the activity (productive). A clever bumper sticker, which read, "I'm very busy doing things I don't need to do in order to avoid doing anything I'm actually supposed to do," indicated the driver, like so many of us, is sacrificing productivity in favor of distractions.

"Busyness" does not equate to "importance" or "meaning." Trying to appear busy in college is a waste of your time and a mistake you will regret later. In contrast, pursuing the good life requires acting with the intention of increasing productivity and well-being. The secret is simultaneously the simplest and the most difficult human activity: pausing our busy lives. It will require you to think consciously about your plans and actions if you are going to be productive. Take a break from the "busyness" to question whether the activities you spend your time on are valuable to you.

PRACTICE AND APPLICATION

Act with Intention

This exercise will help identify actions and activities that contribute to your productivity, well-being, and life satisfaction. More importantly, it will help you identify activities you invest your time in that do not propel you toward a valued goal or are simply ineffective in helping you to accomplish it. Eliminating unimportant activities will reduce busyness and allow you to focus on and enjoy meaningful social activities, leisure time, and self-care without guilt.

Take three minutes each evening this week to mentally review your day. In your notebook, briefly describe one or a few activities you participated in that day. Include activities that you invested considerable time in as well as activities that are shorter or more trivial.

Then, address the following questions for each activity:

1. Why is this activity important? In other words, how does it align with an important objective? This question is critical, but it can be easily misunderstood. Although it may seem that the question

focuses on extrinsic goals like grades or social status, extrinsic goals are secondary and often beyond your control (see chapters 1 and 5). This question refers to intrinsic goals like learning, self-improvement, or well-being, which are in your complete control and aligned with your pursuit of the good life. Incidentally, these intrinsic goals are also essential to achieving good grades and social standing.
2. What motivated you to take part in this activity?
3. Is this activity an effective means to achieve an important goal?
4. Did you enjoy your time while participating in the activity? If you did not, would you have enjoyed the activity if you were not also experiencing anxiety?

Each day, identify and write down in your notebook the activities that are not serving you well and that can safely be cut out of your life. By doing this, you will be able to rededicate your time to more important tasks.

Now write an "implementation intention" to help you avoid those activities during the following day. Implementation intentions, which are strategies proven to improve goal attainment, take the form: "If [*situation*], then I will [*behavior*]." As examples, you could write: If *I feel drawn to scroll social media*, then I will *remind myself that I scroll social media to distract from my exam anxiety*, or then I will *remind myself that scrolling social media doesn't help me learn and slows my progress toward important goals*, or then I will *remind myself that I don't even enjoy scrolling social media*, or then I will *use this time to consider why this exam causes anxiety*.

PURSUIT OF THE GOOD LIFE

It is important that your college experience be enjoyable and that the effort you put into achieving your goals promotes your well-being and satisfaction with life. Many people do not enjoy their time or make consistent progress toward their goals due to dedicating an excessive amount of their free time to unimportant and ineffective activities. In the end, these unimportant activities lead to an overscheduled, busy, frantic, and stressful life. This chapter provides exercises that will help you focus your energy on important and effective tasks by thinking critically about how you choose to spend your unscheduled time. Do not "Just Do It"—the path toward the good life requires you to think about the actions you take and determine if they are worth the effort and time you put into them.

KEY POINTS

- Modern society illogically equates busyness with importance, causing many to overschedule their free time to *appear* busy and thus important.
- Overscheduled people are less productive.
- People focused on productivity do a few important activities that promote progress and improve their well-being; people focused on appearing busy engage in many activities that increase stress without promoting progress or well-being.

CHAPTER SEVEN

EFFECTIVE STUDYING

As she sat at her desk at 3:00 a.m. trying to stay awake, Amara could not believe she was still studying for her philosophy exam that starts in six hours. Furthermore, she has not even read her notes for half of the material that will be covered on the exam, let alone *learned* it well enough to pass. Where had the time gone? She had planned to study every day during the last week, but other events kept getting in the way. First, her friend had an extra ticket to a weekend-long music festival upstate. Amara did not worry about this because there would still be plenty of time to study during the week. The weekend activities left her too tired to study effectively on Monday. Amara knows she is easily distracted and easily frustrated when she attempts to study while tired. She can also admit that scrolling social media until 2:00 a.m. Sunday night was probably a mistake, but she still had the rest of the week to study. She had several classes on Tuesday and some time-consuming homework due next week, but thought, *After I finish this homework, I can focus on studying for the exam.* Amara was unable to effectively utilize the review session on Wednesday because she had not yet studied and most of the questions from the other students were beyond her comprehension. In fact, the review session only heightened her anxiety by making her realize how much she did not know. Amara did not really start studying until Thursday afternoon, and now she feels the stress. *How did this happen?* What really prevented her from studying before Thursday? Looking through her calendar, Amara could recall many times during the week when she thought about studying but chose not to. Why does she continue to make the choice—over and over and over—to wait until the last minute to study?

> *Putting things off is the biggest waste of life: it snatches away each day as it comes, and denies us the present by promising the future.*
> —SENECA[1]

There will always be other activities in which you can participate instead of studying. To be clear, I am *not* suggesting that you never take part in activities outside of the classroom (see chapter 3). In addition to your academic progress, your college experience, well-being, personal growth, and the pursuit of a good life in general rely on nonacademic events and social experiences.[2] The pursuit of non-scholarly interests is an integral part of a fulfilling and meaningful life. But you should ask yourself why you would choose to participate in this specific nonacademic activity. Choosing to spend time on a nonacademic activity that enhances your quality of life or enables you to grow personally is beneficial. However, spending your time on tasks other than academics in order to avoid the psychological or emotional discomfort of studying can be very detrimental. At some point or other, most of us have used nonacademic events to avoid the discomfort of studying.[3] Ancient wisdom suggests it is best to "Concentrate every minute ... on doing what is in front of you with precise and genuine seriousness, tenderly, willingly, with justice. And on freeing yourself from all other distractions."[4] Understanding the reasons for your choice to study or not is vital to understanding the motivations behind your college choices and achieving life satisfaction.

The anxiety and emotional distress associated with difficult course material and exams prevents many students from studying.[5] Studying itself, however, is not difficult. The act of studying simply involves making an effort to read and understand the material presented in class. It is not studying itself that is difficult; it is your thoughts about yourself and your chances of success when you find the material challenging during your studies that is difficult. Studying provokes anxiety and emotional distress since it suggests that you do not know the material and will therefore do poorly on your upcoming exam. That is, study-avoidance behaviors are generally a result of anxiety and emotional distress about failure on the upcoming exam, not a fear of studying or learning the material.[6] As well as being counterproductive, this way of thinking has two notable flaws: it does not follow from logical reasoning and it suggests that your academic success should be measured by exam scores rather than learning.

The purpose of college is to learn new ideas, concepts, and ways of thinking. By definition, the concept of "new" implies that you are not *already* familiar with these ideas. In order to study effectively, you should concentrate most of your time and effort on topics with which you are least comfortable. Spending time on material you already know is not useful. Consequently, you may feel uncomfortable about not understanding most of the material you are spending your time studying.

The psychological distress associated with studying is similar to the lesson we should learn from the stereotypical "dad" story in which he walked to school uphill both ways. Although it is obviously impossible that every dad's trek to school was uphill both ways, there is some truth behind the *feeling* that it was uphill both ways. It probably felt like they had to climb uphill both ways since they dedicated most of their time, effort, and pain to the uphill sections, while coasting pleasurably during the downhill sections. Similarly, the majority of your effort and time should be spent studying the material that you do not understand, while you can coast through the material that you already understand. In light of the fact that you spend most of your time on the more difficult material, it seems reasonable that you *feel* that all of the material is difficult. It is obvious that this is illogical. By all logical reasoning, the most effective way to increase your understanding of material is to focus on what you do not already know well; studying what you already know does not help you and is a waste of time. One way to stop your study-avoidance cycle is to intentionally consider this illogical reasoning whenever you want to postpone studying.[7] The aviator Amelia Earhart once said, "The most difficult thing is the decision to act.... The fears are paper tigers.... You can act to change and control your life; and the procedure, the process is its own reward."[8] Reducing your mental discomfort by questioning the thoughts that lead you to avoid studying will effectively motivate you to study.

The anxiety and psychological distress associated with studying is based on the assumption that exam scores, not learning, determine college success or failure. Although school counselors, professors, other students, and society appear to insist that the point of college is to perform well on exams, it is not. The purpose of higher education is to prepare students with the necessary knowledge base to succeed in their future, not to prepare students to take exams. Exams provide an assessment of how well you have learned the material, but they are arguably minor and even unnecessary tools for achieving the true goal of education. In addition, you do not even have control over how this tool is used; that is, how exams are written and graded.

You do control your effort and your determination to achieve the actual goal of higher education: learning the material. The best way to succeed in higher education is to align your efforts with the true goals of higher education and to focus on activities that are within your control (see the introduction in this book). Changing your perspective about studying—from an unpleasant necessity to improve your grades to an opportunity to learn interesting material that will prepare you for future learning and growth—makes your effort the only metric that determines success (gratifying effort with the goal of learning) or failure (last-minute cramming with the goal of passing an exam). It should be evident that more effective effort will likely result in better exam scores (although you may not focus on your exam grades anymore, better marks are a pleasant side effect of more effective study).

PRACTICE AND APPLICATION

You can dramatically improve your motivation to study if you change the focus of your incentive to study from exam outcomes to learning outcomes. This motivational reframe comes with the added benefits of reduced anxiety, improved well-being, more pleasant experiences while studying, as well as the beneficial byproduct of improved exam scores. Like most of the exercises in this book, reframing your motivations will take practice before they become your automatic response. This week, I recommend spending five to ten minutes each day on the following activities. Performing these practices will help you discover your subconscious thoughts that affect your motivation to study—what you hope to accomplish—and to evaluate if the outcomes you desire are worth your effort (i.e., whether you are motivated by outcomes that are aligned with your values. See chapter 2). If you find these exercises useful, I recommend you practice them during the days and weeks before important exams. Each night, you should answer the following prompts in writing, which will allow you to evaluate your motivations more objectively.

1. Bring an upcoming exam into your mind. Now think about studying the material for this exam within the next ten minutes. What immediate emotions, thoughts, or bodily sensations do you experience when you urge yourself to study? Are these emotions or thoughts indicative of a learning-oriented motivation (positive emotions or thoughts such as excitement, community, or opportunity) or a grade-oriented motivation (negative emotions or thoughts such as fear, anxiety, tiredness, pressure, anger, frustration)?
2. Take a moment to consider the benefits you are likely to achieve if scoring well on the exam is your *only* motivation to study. In other words, what benefits do you expect if you do not care about knowing the material as long as you do well on the exam? Do these benefits align with your values? Is this motivation going to improve your well-being today, in a month, in a year, and in ten years?
3. How likely is it that you will consistently achieve your goal (0–100%) if earning good grades is your ultimate goal? In other words, how often will you be able to achieve the score that you desire on future exams? When your ultimate goal is earning good grades, what is the likelihood that you will consistently achieve life satisfaction and well-being (0–100%)?
4. Now take a moment to consider the benefits of making *learning the material* your only motivation for studying. That is, what benefits do you expect if you are concerned only with increasing your knowledge? Among the benefits could be learning more effectively, spending more time studying, enjoying studying, or even performing well on the exam. Do these benefits align with your values? Is this motivation going to improve your well-being today, in a month, in a year, and in ten years?

5. How likely is it that you will consistently achieve your ultimate goal if you reframe it as a dedicated effort to learn and improve yourself (0–100%)? In other words, how often will studying result in learning more material? What is the probability that you will achieve life satisfaction and well-being if you reframe your ultimate goal into a dedicated effort to learn and to improve yourself (0–100%)?

The only way to guarantee that you achieve your goals—to always get exactly what you want—is to desire only what is within your complete control. Only your effort toward learning the material is under your complete control in most college courses. You can influence your exam scores through your efforts to learn the material, but the professor will also influence your score. The practices above are intended to reinforce the concept that adopting a learning-focused mindset over a grade-focused mindset will improve your well-being and life satisfaction because you always get what you want. You have complete control over your effort to learn the information—the goal of students with a learning-focused mindset—such that getting what you want is entirely within your control. These exercises also reinforce the idea that a learning-focused mindset is better aligned with the primary goals of higher education.

PURSUIT OF THE GOOD LIFE

Reframing your goals to align with a learning-focused mindset will increase your motivation to study. In fact, you may even find studying enjoyable. Maintaining a learning-focused mindset has several additional benefits. First, it is well known that eliminating negative thoughts and emotions around studying, such as anxiety or viewing studying as a chore, results in more effective learning and better retention.[9] Having an interest in the subject makes this benefit even greater. Furthermore, the increased motivation will lead to better study habits, such as studying a little each day rather than waiting until the last minute. In contrast to Amara, who had to cram for her exam, reviewing the material every day results in deeper learning, better recall, and more creative connections between topics. Thus, studying a little every day aligns with the learning-focused mindset. Changing your approach to studying, from a grade-focused to a learning-focused mentality, will result in better exam scores due both to an increase in study efficacy and a decrease in test anxiety (see chapter 8). More importantly, reframing your study goals will allow you to enjoy the time you spend studying while simultaneously progressing toward something that aligns with your values (self-improvement), the very definition of the pursuit of the good life.

KEY POINTS

- Studying provokes anxiety because you concentrate your effort on topics with which you are the least comfortable, which can make you feel like you do not know *any* of the material and will therefore do poorly on your upcoming exam.
- The anxiety caused by studying assumes that exam scores—which are not in your complete control—determine collegiate success; they do not.
- You are in complete control of your efforts to learn the material. Effectively learning the material has the benefit of also improving exam scores.
- Changing your study mindset from a grade-focused to a learning-focused mentality will increase exam scores due both to increased study efficacy and decreased test anxiety.

CHAPTER EIGHT

TEST ANXIETY

Arjun felt prepared for his organic chemistry exam as he headed into the classroom. In addition to studying all week, he attended two review sessions that reassured him that he was studying the correct material, and he took two practice exams on which he scored well. Then the first question on the exam destroyed his confidence. His inability to immediately identify which chemical reaction should occur led to a series of thoughts that spiraled out of control. *How did I not study this? Did I study the wrong material? Will I be able to answer any questions on this exam? It is certain that I will fail this exam! I will need to drop this course and all my plans will be ruined. I will need to take this course during the summer, which will prevent me from participating in the internship program. What does it matter anyway? The internship program will not accept someone who failed organic chemistry. That internship was going to be the cornerstone of my medical school applications, now it's lost! I will be the first person in my family to be rejected from medical school. My father will be so disappointed. He was counting on me to take over his practice. I am such an embarrassment! It is impossible for me to recover from this.* His professor announces that only five minutes remain for him to finish his exam. Although Arjun wrote answers to several of the exam questions, he was distracted by his spiraling thoughts and does not recall thinking about any of them. Dejected, Arjun turns in his exam and prepares himself for the worst.

> *The mind at times fashions for itself false shapes of evil when there are no signs that point to any evil; it twists into the worst construction some word of doubtful meaning . . . [But] there is no limit to our sorrows, if we indulge our fears to the greatest possible extent.*
> —SENECA[1]

That is certainly a lot riding on one organic chemistry exam! Arjun's thought spiral illustrates catastrophizing. Catastrophizing is an all-consuming mental process in which one thought triggers a more dire thought, which provokes still more dire thoughts.[2] Although most of us do not catastrophize at this extreme level, all negative thought spirals adversely affect our performance in the present. There are several aspects of this event to unpack that will allow you to turn Arjun's absurdist exam scenario into a winning test-taking strategy for yourself. To begin with, all the problems that Arjun fears he will face can only occur in the future. The devastating events he foresees are neither currently happening nor have they already occurred. In the present moment, Arjun is fine. In fact, everything seems to be going well for him: he is in a comfortable room, he is not hungry or thirsty, he is healthy, he has a supportive family and a solid group of friends, and he even scored well on an organic chemistry test in the past. As Arjun sits for the exam, he is facing no threats and leading a successful life that most people could only dream of. To paraphrase *Hamlet* and *Seneca*, it is only his thoughts that cause him to feel like life is difficult.

Most approaches to reducing test anxiety, or any anxiety focused on potential future outcomes, begin by deconstructing the feared outcome into its real and improbable components. The overwhelming majority of our anxious thoughts focus on future outcomes that are extremely unlikely to occur.[3] Almost none of Arjun's thoughts, from "I am certainly going to fail this exam" through "I will never recover from this," are supported by any evidence. In fact, nearly all the available evidence suggests that Arjun will do fine on this exam and all exams throughout college. For example, Arjun almost always does well on his exams, providing data that he is likely to do well on this exam as well. Further, Arjun (like you, even if you do not realize it) knows many people who have done very poorly on one or several exams and successfully "recovered"; that is, they graduated from college and have a fulfilling career.

Arjun never questioned the validity of his irrational thoughts, which would crumble under even the slightest scrutiny. Arjun accepted these irrational thoughts as inevitable consequences of failing one exam without further verification. He reached these dubious or even impossible "conclusions" based on untested, and likely untrue, assumptions.

Delusions about some awful future ramifications resulting from minor setbacks in the present are frightening, to put it mildly. But these imagined future calamities are just that, *imagined*.[4] They exist only in your mind and are unlikely to occur in reality.

Questioning feared outcomes, especially the immediate feared outcome (a poor showing on this exam), will reveal that the worst-case scenario is really not that bad, in addition to being highly unlikely. For example, what impact will a poor mark on one organic chemistry exam have on your life? Consider how many students have received a poor mark on an exam and are healthy, with a supportive family and a strong social network; or successfully graduated; or even earned an A in the course? The factual answers to these questions are: almost all, nearly all, and many, respectively. In fact, there are many thousands of successful physicians and scientists, including many professional chemists, who did poorly on at least one science exam in college (I am one of them). I expect that you have not earned perfect scores on every exam you have taken. Even so, you are attending a good college and are well positioned for a successful future. Perhaps you have even thought catastrophically about a past exam whose results did not, in actuality, ruin your life. Most likely, you did not perform as poorly as you imagined and, even if you did, those horrible future scenarios did not occur. Do you still view those prior exams as important today, even though you thought they were *so* important then? A useful technique to counter negative thought spirals is to confront your anxious thoughts with data showing that catastrophes are extremely unlikely based on your past experiences and from the experience of others.

Anxiety associated with exams is future focused, but the exam is taking place now. Anxious thoughts consume part of the processing power of your brain energy, which could otherwise be used to address exam questions.[5] Research suggests that our working memory—the amount of information we can actively process in a single moment—is incredibly limited.[6] The average person can process only seven bits of information at any given time.[7] Using any of your brain's processing power on anxious thoughts will limit your effectiveness on the exam. You have likely experienced a similar phenomenon if you tend to perform better when the stakes are low, such as during rehearsal or on practice exams, suggesting that anxiety decreases your effectiveness. Overall, anxious thoughts both reduce your sense of well-being in the present moment *and* impair your performance on exams.

Self-improvement, not grades, is the primary objective for students in college (see chapter 7). The purpose of studying academic topics is to become better educated and to build the foundation for future career opportunities (if these are not your goals, please refer to chapters 1 and 2). No part of becoming better educated is improved by considering exam outcomes. In the same way as described above, worrying about exams is likely to hinder your educational progress.[8] Outcome-driven approaches cause anxiety because these performance metrics are partially beyond your control. Furthermore, they provide you with the data you need to compare yourself to others, to feel judged, and to harshly judge yourself.

Students who adopt a learning-focused approach can avoid anxious thoughts because this approach values effort and progress, not outcomes. The only thing that determines your progress and self-improvement is your effort. Additionally, a learning-focused approach does not provide you with data to compare your success with others or to feel judged. Students who employ a learning-focused approach have numerous advantages over students who employ an exam-focused approach, both in terms of well-being and traditional metrics of success. First, learning is a process where each step adds to your knowledge base and is completely under your control—you are in complete control of your effort and thus in complete control of your level of "success." Second, eliminating the possibility of judgment, comparisons, and metrics of success and failure limits anxious thoughts and allows you to focus more effectively on your exam (see chapter 9). The learning-focused approach is more appropriate even in courses graded on a curve, since focusing on your own learning—which you control—improves your score, while anxious thoughts about the scores of other students—which you cannot control—are a distraction that negatively affects your own score. Accordingly, learning-focused students achieve better exam outcomes than exam-focused students,[9] although the outcome may not matter to the purely learning-focused student. By approaching your many college exams with a learning-based mindset, you will achieve greater well-being and life satisfaction, as well as better results on exams. The process of becoming a learning-focused student is easier said than done. In the following sections, you will find techniques to help you overcome test anxiety in the present, as well as exercises that will help you change your mindset to become more learning-focused in the future.

PRACTICE AND APPLICATION

Preparation is the key to reducing the impact of test anxiety. These techniques provide a blueprint for coping with test anxiety on exam day. Moreover, there are multiple preparatory approaches described that you can practice in order to "unlearn" your current focus on exam outcomes, to limit future test anxiety, and to develop your learning-focused mindset.

1. Take a Pause

The first thing you need to do to combat anxious thoughts is to stop whatever you are doing. This step is essential when you are studying as well as when you are sitting for an exam. Focus your thoughts by taking a brief, calming pause. A common technique is to take two to five deep breaths (inhale for two to four seconds; hold for four seconds; exhale for five to six seconds), focusing on the sensation of the air filling and escaping your lungs. This technique, which you may recognize from modern mindfulness practices, focuses your mind on the present moment, helps you to gain emotional distance, and can temporarily break the destructive thought spiral associated with test anxiety. Another useful technique, eye movement desensitization and reprocessing (EMDR) therapy, or the "eye scramble," disrupts anxious thoughts by making it difficult for you to keep them in focus. Simply move your eyes in random directions without moving your head for five to ten seconds. This modern psychological technique used for treating patients with PTSD can be very effective at breaking negative thought spirals.[10] The remaining steps should be practiced prior to your exam.

2. Deconstruct the Object of Your Anxious Thoughts

Once you have temporarily exited the catastrophizing thought spiral, categorize the negative thoughts into those that are factual and those that are improbable and likely driven by fear. To do this, write your anxious thoughts in brief, simple, and unemotional language. For example, the statement "Failing this exam will be a disaster" describes both the feared event and the emotional reaction, whereas the statement "I will fail this exam" describes only the feared event; choose the latter.

Now read each statement and mark it as accurate (objectively true) or inaccurate/improbable. To determine the accuracy and probability of the statements, use your past experience or the experience of others you know. As an example, you have passed and likely performed quite well on most of your past exams, indicating that you will likely do well on this upcoming exam. In your notebook, revise each inaccurate or improbable statement into a statement that is 100 percent correct. As an example, you could modify "I will fail this exam" to "Given my prior record, there is almost no chance that I will fail this exam." It is essential to remain factually accurate. However, preventing your emotions from clouding your judgment and remaining factually accurate is very difficult and will take time to learn. If you find yourself trending toward a negative thought spiral—no problem—revisit step 1.

3. How Likely Is It Really?

Estimate the probability that each of the factual statements written above will actually happen. In your notebook, describe any evidence suggesting the feared outcome is likely to occur. Make a fair assessment by also describing the evidence that suggests the feared outcome will not happen or that a different outcome is more likely. The most useful data often comes from your own experiences. For example, did previous exams that gave you anxiety turn out as poorly as you had anticipated? There is no doubt that you did better on most of these exams than your anxious thoughts suggested, providing irrefutable evidence that your current anxious thoughts are also unfounded. In addition, it can be helpful to describe the data supporting the most probable outcomes, such as, "I am likely to do well on this exam," which is much more probable than the outcome you fear anyway.

In an anxious state, the brain concentrates so hard on the worst-case scenario that it fails to question the likelihood that the worst-case scenario will actually occur. If the probability of the worst case occurring is vanishingly small, you can safely ignore it. If you recognize these anxious thoughts in your head, remind yourself (gently) that they are only thoughts, and that the catastrophe is very unlikely to happen. Do not be frustrated when these thoughts return. Just repeat the exercises in steps 2 and 3.

In the event that you feel anxious during the exam, take a pause and then remind yourself that the object of your anxiety is unlikely. In addition, it may be helpful to include a description of the most likely alternative, nonanxiety-provoking outcome in this reminder. You may want to write this reminder on scratch paper before the exam starts and read it to yourself if you feel anxious.

4. Determine How Any of the Statements in Step 2 Actually Impact Your Life

Even if some of the outcomes in your anxious thoughts do occur, they may have little impact on your life and are thus not worth worrying about. The following are two techniques designed to reduce anxiety levels and increase feelings of well-being by examining the possible impact of outcomes you consider negative.

(a) Put the feared outcome in a broader context. By contextualizing your thoughts, you can recognize that negative events have only a limited impact. For example, there are many people who have failed exams, some of whom you may know personally (even if they have not told you), who are currently happy, healthy, and successful in their careers. Their exam difficulties had little impact on their careers or personal lives. Similarly, your upcoming exam will likely have only a small impact on your life, regardless of the grade you receive. Your score on this exam may not even have a large impact on your course grade! Taking into account that any outcome on the exam should only have a minor impact on your life, you can safely confirm that there is no cause for anxiety. Use your notebook to put each of the feared outcomes from step 2 into a broader context. Note how, in the grand scheme of things, very little will change based on the results of one exam. Remind yourself of this if you feel anxious during an exam.

(b) Give yourself advice. What advice would you give your friends if they were worried about failing an exam? As a result of your emotional

distance from the situation, you will be more likely to correctly observe that they will likely perform well on the exam, just as they generally do (and you generally do, too). Further, you will recognize that the actual impact of receiving one poor exam score on their life is really not that bad. While maintaining this emotional distance, write a note of advice to yourself about your upcoming exam as if you were advising a friend. As this is a note from another person to you, use your first name throughout the letter when addressing the recipient. This exercise will enable you to gain the emotional distance you need to objectively evaluate the impact of feared outcomes on your life. It is recommended that you take this letter with you to your exam if your professor permits you to do so.

5. What Is the Point?

Consider whether your current anxiety is helping you right now. That is, how does worrying help you in the present moment? There are few circumstances in our modern society in which anxiety will improve your performance, and anxiety will generally have a negative effect. When you feel anxious, remind yourself that anxious thoughts are not helpful. If you notice anxious thoughts while studying or taking an exam, take a moment to jot them down. Promise yourself that you will give these anxious thoughts your full attention after the exam. By promising yourself the space to process these thoughts at a more convenient time, you will be more likely to put them aside so that you can concentrate on your exam. In your notebook, describe how your anxious thoughts help or hinder your well-being and ability to perform well on your exam. Seeing how anxiety negatively impacts your life in black and white can help you put your logic back in control and reduce the impact of your emotional thinking.

PURSUIT OF THE GOOD LIFE

Exams can be one of the most stressful parts of college life, but they do not have to be. The anxiety associated with exams has nothing to do with self-improvement or learning the material. Test anxiety is rarely even about the exam itself. In most cases, test anxiety stems from the incorrect assumption that a poor performance on this exam will create disastrous consequences for your future. In reality, it is unlikely that you will face the calamities you fear even if you receive a poor mark. Moreover, the poor score you fear rarely occurs. The majority of students do much better than they expected. Even those who experience a poor exam score often do well in their courses, majors, and careers. The strategies presented in this chapter can help you reduce test anxiety during your college career. It will, however, require repeated practice to unlearn old habits and to acquire better ones. In many cases, seeking professional help through campus resources can speed your progress toward reducing test anxiety (see chapter 10). Although reducing your anxiety around exams takes effort, it is worth the effort. A reduced level of test anxiety will have a positive impact on many aspects of your college experience, including more efficient learning and better performance on exams. Most importantly, progress toward limiting anxiety is progress in the pursuit of the good life.

KEY POINTS

- Anxious thoughts focus on future outcomes that are often extremely unlikely to occur.
- Anxious thoughts consume brain power that could be used to address exam questions, thus limiting your effectiveness on the exam. Anxious thoughts reduce well-being in the present moment *and* result in worse exam performance.
- Adopting a learning-focused approach will exclude anxious thoughts, as this approach values effort and progress, not exam outcomes. Learning-focused students achieve better exam outcomes than exam-focused students.

CHAPTER NINE

COMPETITIVE PEERS

Omar is convinced that he is the worst student in all his courses. The other students constantly talk about how much they study, how well they do in their courses, and how interesting and important their extracurricular activities are. Omar believes that his peers look down on him whenever he asks questions about course material or does not recognize the *extreme importance* of the activities they boast about. In addition, at least one student in each of his courses is determined to demonstrate that they already know all the information presented in the course and even some from more advanced courses. These students frequently dominate class time with esoteric questions about related but irrelevant topics. What can Omar do to compete with his classmates who already know so much and participate in so many extracurricular activities?

> *If you want to improve, be content to be thought foolish and stupid with regard to external things. Do not wish to be thought to know anything.*
> —EPICTETUS[1]

Competition among students, and among people in general, is a regrettable reality. Despite appearances to the contrary, both students who boast about their achievements and those who feel they are underperforming by comparison suffer from uncertainty about their self-image (see chapter 2). The boasters exaggerate their accomplishments in order to gain the attention, praise, and recognition they need to maintain their projected self-image.[2] The students who compare their success to the exaggerated stories of the boaster feel inferior and less respected. As author and lifestyle guru Timothy Ferriss notes, "If you are insecure, guess what? The rest of the world is too. Do not overestimate the competition and underestimate yourself. You are better than you think."[3]

The desire for respect from our peers likely evolved in our hunter-gatherer ancestors to increase our chances of remaining in social groups that offered protection, food, and mates.[4] Historically, those ancestors who did not contribute to the prosperity of their group were abandoned and left to protect themselves from predators and competing social groups. In the modern world, it is not the innate desire to feel respected, needed, or valued that is problematic. It is problematic in modern societies to allow others to decide what activities and accomplishments are worthy of respect, as it negatively impacts your well-being and life satisfaction. Ironically, it also negatively impacts your academic and career success.

The actions and thoughts of both the boasting student and the student dispirited by the boasting are motivated by the desire to maintain or enhance their projected image (the boaster) or their self-image (the dispirited student feeling inferior by comparison). A projected image represents how you want your peers and professors to view you, a means of demonstrating your "value" to the group.[5] Projecting an exaggerated or even fabricated image, however, is counterproductive to learning and self-improvement. In addition to being energy intensive to maintain, exaggerated projected images can prevent students from participating in the activities that will help them progress toward their academic goals. For example, it is impossible for students to demonstrate that they already know all the course material (an exaggerated projected image) while simultaneously asking questions about material they do not yet understand (the primary goal of college courses). Thus, students who exaggerate their accomplishments will find it extremely difficult to become the person they are already claiming to be.

Projecting an exaggerated image of success has few benefits, but many negative consequences. Students who highlight their own accomplishments are seeking praise to ease their insecurities, but they rarely receive praise from peers or professors. These students' insecurities increase when their success stories are not acknowledged or praised, which causes them to seek praise more aggressively.[6] Unfortunately for the praise-seeking student, everyone in the class, including the professor, can quickly recognize the disconnect between what the student knows and what they want others to think they know. Eventually, these boastful students realize that no one accepts the exaggerated image they are trying to present. They may even perceive a growing animosity from their peers, which can exacerbate their insecurities still further. Taking into consideration the pitiable mindsets of these students can eliminate the negative effects their boasting may have had on your psychological well-being.

There are also few benefits to comparing yourself to other students, and there are many disadvantages as well. Comparing yourself to others suggests the painful and distracting interpretation that you are not as capable and therefore less likely to succeed than your peers.[7] This interpretation, however, is rarely accurate since it is based on *exaggerated* stories of success. The psychological distress caused by erroneous peer comparisons limits your capacity to learn new information, which is the primary goal of your courses. It is important to emphasize that you should *not* already know the material before taking the course. What is the point of wasting your time studying material you already know? It should not be surprising or upsetting if a student who has already learned the material understands it better than you do. It is more rational to feel pity for students who demonstrate their *advanced* knowledge, since they are wasting time and money for no other reason than to support their egos. Remember that "It is silly to try to escape other people's faults. They are inescapable. Just try to escape your own."[8]

The successes (real or exaggerated) of fellow students do not prevent you from learning the material. That is, whether you appear more or less capable than your peers is not an accurate measure of your capacity as a student, nor of your ability to learn, nor what mark you will earn in the course. The reality is that there will always be someone "better" somewhere on earth, but this hasn't stopped the remaining 7.89 billion of us from being successful and pursuing the good life. Being the "best" is not a reasonable goal; doing your best while enjoying life will lead to success and is aligned with the pursuit of the good life. The act of comparing yourself to your peers provides you with few benefits and negatively impacts your mental health, motivation, and ability to learn.[9] The exercises below will help you recognize and break free of the idea that your value is determined by how well you perform compared to your peers. In reality, you are valued by the degree to which you strive to meet principled goals such as learning, improving oneself and society, and maintaining an ethical lifestyle.

PRACTICE AND APPLICATION

There will always be students that attempt to demonstrate their importance by describing (and often exaggerating) their achievements, broadcasting their knowledge, or deriding your achievements. It is impossible for you to control what they do, but you can control how you react to what they do. One strategy is to consider why these students engage in competitive behaviors. In other words, shift your focus from "How does their behavior affect me?" to "Why do they behave this way?" This perspective change will alleviate negative reflections about your own performance and generate compassion for your self-conscious peers. In most cases, these behaviors are motivated by a sense of insecurity about how you and the professor perceive their capacity as a student. This state of mind merits compassion and pity, not scorn. Use the following prompts to reframe your response to boastful students in your notebook.

- How do these students benefit from boasting about their achievements or making derogatory remarks about others?
- What is your classmate likely thinking and feeling before, during, and after a boastful or derogatory comment?
- How would you react to a small child who made similar boastful or derogatory remarks? With compassion or with anger?
- Would your perception of your own capabilities change if a small child made similar boastful or derogatory remarks? Would these remarks cause you any mental distress?

I expect that these types of boastful or derogatory statements you hear from classmates would not bother you if they came from a child.

I expect you might even find it amusing that a child, who has no understanding of their abilities yet still wants to feel significant, would be so bold. The reason you are not bothered by it is that the child's words are obviously inaccurate and they do not affect you, unless you let them. The words and behaviors of your boastful classmate are no different. Similar to the child, your classmate is acting from a place of insecurity and misunderstanding of themselves and the world. Their words have no effect on you or your life, unless you let them. As this kind of behavior from a small child would not affect you, there is no reason to let similar behaviors from your classmates have any impact on you.

In addition to impacting your well-being, competitive students can be disruptive and impact your ability to learn. If a student's tangential questions, intended to demonstrate their *vast* knowledge, result in a disjointed and confusing lecture, you should let the professor know after class. Please believe me when I tell you that your professors find these students and the situations they create extremely difficult as well. In my courses, I appreciate students expressing concerns about these challenging students, as it indicates that I have assessed the situation correctly. Furthermore, I am much more likely to confront boastful students if I know that their behavior is negatively affecting the learning experience of other students than if I thought it only annoyed me.

You can use your notebook to write out the points you want to convey to your professor. This will make your conversation shorter, more relevant, and more efficient. You will be most effective if you remain calm and stick to the facts without embellishment or showing frustration during your discussion with the professor. Remember that you do not control how your professor handles this situation. Once you have clearly stated the issues you are facing as a student, it is in your interest to allow the professor to address the problems in their class and to concentrate on learning the material.

Overly competitive students regularly impact the mental well-being of their peers, and rarely in a positive way. The good news is that these students can only impact your mental well-being if you allow them to. You can challenge the accuracy of comparisons that occur (internally, do not address the boaster) and refrain from initiating peer comparisons. Remember that you will not gain any benefits and will suffer many disadvantages if you evaluate your success in relation to that of your peers. College is a time for learning and self-improvement; peer comparisons and aiming to meet the standards of success defined by a loud minority of boastful students will not help. How much time other students spend studying, how well they perform on exams, what they do with their spare time, or any other standard they try to establish is not relevant to your success. Comparing yourself to your peers can lead you to think that you are struggling more than your peers, that you are less capable, and that you have a lower probability of success. In nearly every case, these negative feelings are not based on accurate information, but can crush your desire to learn, your motivation, and even your capacity to succeed.

In your notebook, write a brief description of a time when you engaged in peer comparison. The event could be a reaction to an overly competitive student's statement or an unprompted comparison to another student.

If you can recall, write a description of how this event affected your motivation to learn and your well-being. For example, did this event negatively impact your well-being or life satisfaction and were you more distracted or less motivated in this course after the event?

In your notebook, consider the advantages and disadvantages of peer comparison. That is, was it worth the mental and emotional effort to engage in a peer comparison?

You can refer to this exercise whenever you find yourself comparing your achievements or potential achievements with those of your classmates in the future.

Avoid interacting with competitive students whenever possible. It may not be possible to avoid interactions with disheartening students entirely, but you should try to do so as often as possible. Most students, if given the choice, would choose to focus on learning the material without worrying about "who is the best." Whenever possible, simply excuse yourself from situations in which you will have to interact with any of the vocal minority of students that boast and bluster. Similarly, make an effort to interact with classmates who share your study habits, academic goals, and values (see chapter 2).

PURSUIT OF THE GOOD LIFE

There are no benefits to peer comparisons. They do, however, reduce your life satisfaction and impede your progress toward your goals. Comparing yourself to others is most likely to negatively impact your sense of well-being and distract you from learning and improving yourself. Removing unnecessary distractions such as peer competition will increase your capacity to learn the material and thus increase your chances of earning better exam scores—possibly higher marks than the braggadocios in your course (though such a comparison would be more detrimental than helpful). Students who are overly competitive may seem common, but they are actually a small but loud minority. Avoiding these students and finding students who will support and celebrate your progress, will help you eliminate the negative impacts of peer competition, increase your joy of learning, and aid you in your pursuit of the good life in college.

KEY POINTS

- Peer comparisons—which can erroneously suggest that you are not as capable as your peers—limit your capacity to learn and negatively impact your well-being and life satisfaction.
- There will always be students who exaggerate their achievements or belittle yours in order to ease their insecurities.
- Proclaiming your own successes to demonstrate your "value" is energy intensive and will prevent you from participating in the activities that will help you achieve the very success you proclaim.
- *Appearing* capable is an inaccurate measure of your capacity as a student, your ability to learn, or what mark you will earn in the course.

CHAPTER TEN

ASK FOR GUIDANCE

"I should have just asked for help," Matteo tells himself. Matteo recalls his mother scolding his father every time they got lost, "Why don't you just stop and ask for directions?" The fact that Matteo is becoming his father is the least of his concerns at the moment. Matteo's courses this semester have been difficult because the material is challenging and because the instructions for the assignments are often unclear. Matteo, like his father, is uncomfortable asking for clarification on assignments or material. Rather than asking for help, Matteo spends hours trying to understand what he is supposed to do and still regularly turns in assignments that he completed incorrectly. Moreover, he frequently studies concepts that he interpreted incorrectly, further cementing his misunderstanding of course material. Having fallen behind in several courses by midsemester only exacerbated his anxiety about seeking help with the material or for general guidance. Matteo believes that his professors would scoff at his requests because he is not performing well in their classes. At this point, Matteo does not know where to find the help and guidance he needs. He does not even know who can help him begin his search. The barriers to seeking help, including his own discomfort and his unfamiliarity with the support services at his university, seem too high to overcome. Matteo feels stuck and has no idea how to change his strategy to succeed this semester.

> *To know that one knows what one knows, and to know that one does not know what one does not know, there lies true wisdom.*
> —CONFUCIUS[1]

Many college campuses provide services designed to enhance the learning experience of students as well as services to improve student well-being and the overall experience of undergraduates. In addition to the professors and teaching assistants in your courses—whose explicit purpose is to educate students—there are often learning centers to develop study skills, peer tutors for many classes, medical services, mental health services, financial services, and many other services. Just as you would seek help from a physician for a medical issue without a second thought, you should seek help for anything that can improve your learning, mental health, well-being, or overall experience. As an extension of this analogy, just as you should visit your physician for annual checkups even when you are not experiencing medical issues, you should regularly make use of any other service that will help you maintain a high quality of life. In the worst-case scenario, you might find that your campus does not provide the service you need, although this is highly unlikely. Even in this unlikely worst-case scenario, however, you would be no worse off than you would be if you did not seek help.

In many cases, students are hesitant to ask for help because they are unclear about what type of assistance would be beneficial. A controversial US secretary of defense once paraphrased Confucius, saying, "There are known knowns. These are things we know that we know. There are known unknowns. That is to say, there are things that we know we don't know. But there are also unknown unknowns. There are things we don't know we don't know."[2] There are many novel challenges that college students face that they cannot fully describe, categorize, or even recognize as challenges. These are the "unknown unknowns." It is nearly impossible to determine what kind of assistance will be useful if the problem is not clearly defined.

Every journey toward self-improvement involves unidentifiable problems since these experiences are always fundamentally new to you. This is not bad news. It is likely that your university has services dedicated to addressing any problems you may be experiencing, as millions of students have experienced similar issues. It is just a matter of finding the correct person or office. Often, finding the appropriate resource requires asking a professor, adviser, or trusted peer who will refer you to a less-than-perfect person or office, where you will then be directed to the relevant person. The cost of contacting two or three offices in search of appropriate guidance is minimal, while the benefit is substantial. Many students, like Matteo, make the mistake of never asking for help, while many other students abandon their search one step too early.[3]

When you consider how common many of these issues are, you may wonder why it often takes multiple steps to find the appropriate resources. Even though college campuses almost always offer the services you need, these services are rarely organized into an easy-to-navigate catalog. Most campuses have no centralized office that is even aware of all the services available to undergraduates. Further, it is not uncommon for multiple organizations on campus to provide similar services. There is a common misconception that having more options is beneficial. However, research suggests that too many choices can lead to anxiety about making an incorrect choice, which inhibits students from engaging any service.[4] Poor organization or the absence of easily accessible information about student services is not within your control. However, seeking appropriate services is within your control and is crucial to your well-being and life satisfaction.

The false belief that asking for help means admitting that you are not capable of being successful on your own is a formidable obstacle to seeking help or guidance.[5] A number of logical flaws are present in this belief. The most important thing to remember is that no one has ever succeeded without the help of others. The decision to attend college is, by definition, a decision to seek the guidance you need to achieve your educational goals. That is, when you choose to attend college, you admit that you do not yet possess the skills or knowledge required to achieve your goals and that you cannot gain this knowledge without the assistance of your professors. The process of seeking additional guidance to improve your capacity to learn or improve in some other way while you are in college is not fundamentally different. It can, however, *feel* different because of peer comparisons (see chapter 9) or due to perceived damage to your self-image as "smart" or as a good student (see chapter 2). As an example, students may mistakenly assume they are a worse student because other students do not require additional help to succeed (but see the following paragraph). Feelings of comparative inadequacy, vulnerability, and stigma associated with seeking help keep many students from seeking the guidance that would improve their educational effectiveness and their overall college experience. Do not let your (likely incorrect) assumptions about the opinions of others dissuade you from seeking the help and guidance that will benefit your life in college.

It is a surprisingly well-kept secret that students who understand the college system, often through family with prior college experience, are more likely to use the resources available to them. Further, many students who are doing well in their classes regularly use learning centers, tutors, and office hours.[6] It is my experience that most A students in my courses regularly attend office hours, whereas C students rarely do. In the same way, people who are not currently experiencing a mental health crisis regularly visit a therapist, just like people who are not currently sick or injured get medical checkups and those without cavities visit their dentist. Seeking help and guidance is not about *needing* help or guidance; it is simply using the available resources to maximize your potential, improve your mental health and well-being, enhance your overall experience, and support your pursuit of the good life.[7] As the civil rights activist César Chávez[8] correctly identified, "You are never strong enough that you don't need help." The student resources on your campus can make your life better. *Use them!* That is why they exist.

Overcoming the mental barriers that are preventing you from seeking guidance or help requires that you assess your internal dialogue about what asking for help "means" about you. Hint: it does not *mean* anything.[9] The stigma you associate with asking for help is rooted in your innate instinct to impress your peers and professors.[10] Put another way, your belief that what others think about you, how they judge you, and what they value about you is more important than your learning, self-improvement, and well-being. These concerns about others' opinions of you can prevent you from seeking the guidance or help that will enhance your college experience. Many techniques can be used to address these thoughts, some of which can be found in chapters 2, 4, and 9, in addition to the exercises presented below. The techniques in this chapter are built on three principles: (1) asking for help is in your complete control; (2) what others think about you is not in your control and cannot affect your life unless you allow it to; and (3) caring or not caring about what others think of you is in your complete control.

PRACTICE AND APPLICATION

The purpose of the practices in this chapter is incredibly straightforward—learn to ask for help whether or not you think you need it. The worst thing that can happen is that you do not immediately find the resources you are seeking. However, you will undoubtedly come across resources that will prove helpful to yourself or your friends at some point during college. I would like to encourage you to immediately identify and map out the resources available to undergraduates at your college aimed at improving study skills, mental health and well-being, and your overall experience. Engaging the learning resources at the beginning of every semester is also beneficial to you. For example, you should set up regular sessions with the tutor assigned to your courses at the beginning of the semester, even though you do not yet *need* any help. Engaging these resources early in the semester can only enhance your learning process and improve your life at very little cost to your time or effort. By identifying and utilizing these resources now, you will also gain the experience necessary to make the most of them when they are actually needed.

What You Will Need to Ask for Help

The only action that must be taken is to overcome the mental and emotional barriers that stigmatize seeking help. You can do this most productively by asking yourself what asking for help means about you and your capabilities. In reality, seeking guidance only means that you are trying to take advantage of the available resources to improve yourself and your experience. Using the available resources is no different from selecting the instructors or coaches who are most capable of providing the guidance you need to improve. Utilizing available resources does not reflect negatively on your character or indicate that you are less competent than those who do not take advantage of the available resources. A negative self-judgment or anxiety about possible opinions from peers or professors is irrational and unwarranted. You may find these ideas easy to comprehend rationally, but accepting and applying them to your life will involve practice. To help you to put these judgments and anxieties into a more realistic perspective, write in your notebook what you would think of a *friend* who needed help.

Now address the same question about yourself in your notebook. What would you think about yourself if you sought additional help to make your progress easier? Make sure you treat yourself with as much respect and kindness as you would a friend.

Now describe how finding effective guidance would impact your education, well-being, and life satisfaction. In other words, if you found the guidance useful and it improved your life.

The process of personal improvement requires both your own effort and the assistance of others. The fact that you receive help does not detract from your accomplishments any more than taking a course to guide you in a specific academic subject. Guidance is guidance, effort is effort, and both are necessary for your success and for life satisfaction.

What You *Do Not* Need before Seeking Help

BEING PREPARED

Many students skip review sessions, office hours, or therapy sessions because they believe they have not prepared themselves well enough. Although better preparation may enable you to make better use of these sessions, do not let inadequate preparation stop you from participating. Engaging in the available resources will still help you to improve even if you are underprepared. If you arrive unprepared, you may feel that you will look foolish or that the professor or therapist will be offended that you wasted their time. Generally, this is not true. More importantly, it is not your problem. The way you make use of an available resource is your business and the only thing you can control.

You should not take over a review session by asking all the questions, but there is no reason not to attend and ask some questions. You will be surprised by how many other students have the same question, even if they were better prepared. It is not necessary that you know everything when you attend a review session or office hours. Review sessions and office hours are meant to clarify concepts that students do not understand. Providing students with a resource that teaches material that every student already knows would be a waste of time for a professor. The excuses students often make, which generally rest on incorrect assumptions about what they need to accomplish prior to making use of resources, are a major obstacle to engaging in helpful services. List the excuses you have made to avoid attending a review session or seeking assistance, as shown in the left column of the example that follows. In the right column, analyze the credibility of those excuses. You will be better prepared to accept the reality of your assessment about how prepared you need to be if you describe how these excuses have hindered your educational progress and well-being.

MY EXCUSE	THE REALITY
The professor will be annoyed if I ask a dumb question during office hours.	The point of office hours is to clarify misunderstandings about the course material. The professor wants us to ask questions about what we do not understand. I will be less likely to learn and will not feel good about my progress if I do not attend office hours.

Who to Ask and Where to Go for Help

There is no reason that you should know who or where to turn for help or guidance. The best advice is to ask anyone you think might be able to guide you in the right direction if you need assistance. The worst that can happen is that they will not know and you will need to ask someone else. You can ask anyone on the faculty, staff, or even another student you trust. It is possible that the person you initially ask will not be able to provide the assistance you need. However, they are likely to refer you to someone who can. My advice: ask for advice whether you think you need it or not.

PURSUIT OF THE GOOD LIFE

Your educational and personal progress can only be enhanced by seeking help and guidance. In reality, it is never detrimental to seek help, but it can be damaging if you *believe* untrue self-critical beliefs about what it *means* to seek help or guidance. The process of seeking help means that you are using the available resource to improve yourself, your learning, or your well-being. It has nothing to do with your ability to succeed. Nevertheless, the stigma that many students associate with seeking help could prevent you from taking advantage of the available resources that can help guide you on your pursuit of the good life in college. The key is to seek help and ignore all other mental obstacles. Ensure that you evaluate whether the guidance (including the advice in this book) is helpful and choose to follow the advice that works for you. Do not be discouraged if any particular advice does not work for you. Not every technique works for everyone at every stage of their lives. Simply continue to seek additional guidance until you discover what works for you in your pursuit of the good life.

KEY POINTS

- An intimidating obstacle to seeking help or guidance for many students is the incorrect belief that asking for help is admitting that they are incapable of success on their own. However, no one has ever succeeded without help from others.
- The majority of students using student services do not *need* help; they are simply using the available resources to maximize their academic potential, mental health and well-being, and overall experience.
- Your campus likely has the services necessary to address any undergraduate issue, although it may be necessary to contact two or more offices in search of appropriate guidance.
- Seeking appropriate services is within your complete control and is crucial to your well-being, life satisfaction, and academic and career success.

CHAPTER ELEVEN

GRADE UNCERTAINTY

After submitting her midsemester project, Sauna still does not know whether she is doing well in her European history course. The subject interests her and she has been doing everything she can to learn the material. She attends every lecture, regularly attends office hours, reviews her notes and reads the assigned chapters, and participates in her weekly study group. Nevertheless, this midsemester project is the first of only two graded projects, and the professor has not provided a grading rubric describing the criteria for judging the project. It is eight weeks into the semester, and she cannot predict whether she will earn an A, a C, or if she will even pass the course. Further, there is no one she can ask about her performance in the class—even the professor does not know this yet. Since the withdrawal date has passed, she cannot withdraw from the course if she did not perform well on the midsemester project. As there have been no evaluations, Sauna does not even know if she understands the material. She wonders if her sustained effort to learn the material has been a waste of time. She is consumed with anxiety about the uncertain nature of her grade in the course. In spite of this, there is nothing she can do to reduce the uncertainty. So all she does is worry, and she does it constantly.

> *Nothing gives a person so much*
> *advantage over another as to remain always cool*
> *and unruffled under all circumstances.*
> —THOMAS JEFFERSON[1]

The design of the majority of college courses leaves students unsure of their potential grade throughout the semester. The majority of course grades are determined by a few major exams or projects, and poor performance on any one of them can significantly affect your grade. It is even common for courses with many graded assignments—quizzes, graded homework, participation, and so forth—to have a final exam that accounts for 25 to 50 percent of the final grade. As a result, even if you have performed well throughout the semester, you are unlikely to be able to predict your final grade before the semester ends. Because of the limited number of evaluations, students motivated by self-improvement rather than grades may also feel uncertain about their progress in learning the material (see chapter 5). That is, learning-focused students may be unsure whether the concepts they are learning match those the professor is trying to convey. Grade uncertainty and learning-focused uncertainty are both common sources of discomfort for students.[2] The most effective strategy for maintaining your well-being and improving your academic performance is to acquire the ability to accept and find calm in uncertainty—the focus of this chapter.

It is unclear why so few evaluations are used in most college courses. This common course design may be inherited from a historical style of education, or it may be the result of active research that has determined that this is the best educational approach for college courses, or it could simply be a desire by professors to spend less time grading (grading is the most unpleasant part of teaching!). No matter the underlying rationale, most courses use few evaluations, and students cannot influence course design. You can, however, control your response to the uncertainty that accompanies courses that use a small number of crucial evaluations. You have two, admittedly patronizing-sounding, options: (a) to let the uncertainty bother you or (b) to *not* let the uncertainty bother you.

Allowing the uncertainty to bother you almost never increases your chances of a positive outcome and often makes things worse.[3] Even though you may be correct that there is no rational justification for a course design that provokes anxiety in so many students, displaying your righteous anger will not change the course design for at least two reasons. First, due to the planning necessary to effectively administer a course, your professor cannot alter the design during the semester regardless of your level of dissatisfaction. Second, a rational and convincing argument could persuade your professor to change the course design for future semesters. However, appearing upset makes your arguments appear more emotional than logical, which will undermine the effectiveness of your arguments.[4] As Plato is credited with suggesting, "There are two things a person should never be angry at, what they can control, and what they cannot." That is, anger will not help in situations over which you have no control nor in situations over which you have control.

Allowing the uncertainty to bother you is also likely to decrease your well-being, life satisfaction, and educational success. As an example, getting upset over grade uncertainty will exacerbate your anxiety, which will negatively affect your course grade (see chapters 7 and 8). Furthermore, being upset will waste mental energy that could otherwise be used for learning the material or other productive pursuits (see chapter 5). Your righteous anger could also lead you to act unproductively if you allow it to intensify. In total, righteous anger will not change the design of your course and is likely to negatively affect your life. This type of righteous anger is similar to angrily hitting your computer when the internet is failing; it will not cause the internet to recover, your computer is unlikely to apologize for failing you, your computer may get damaged, you will not feel any better, and you will probably feel foolish.

Not allowing uncertainty to bother you, by contrast, will always increase your well-being and will often lead to improved academic progress and better grades. Ancient wisdom recognizes that "To bear trials with a calm mind robs misfortune of its strength and burden."[5] The most effective strategy for overcoming obstacles and achieving your goals is to approach difficult situations calmly and rationally.[6] Putting this strategy into practice, however, is not easy. The exercises detailed below are designed to help you develop a set of skills to investigate the true impact of uncertainty on your life and to alleviate the associated anxiety. Accepting uncertainty as an inevitable part of life is the first step toward reducing uncertainty-associated anxiety. Math professor and author John Allen Paulos writes, "Uncertainty is the only certainty there is, and knowing how to live with insecurity is the only security."[7] By accepting that grade uncertainty remains until the end of the semester—rather than indulging in righteous anger or wallowing in anxiety—you can eliminate the impact grade uncertainty has on you. By accepting that you cannot change the course design, you can concentrate on more productive pursuits that are under your complete control, such as studying and leisure activities.

The anxiety-provoking uncertainty caused by college courses is almost always associated with grade outcomes and rarely with the process of learning the material. Although your final grade and exam scores are not entirely within your complete control, you are in complete control of how much effort you put into learning the material. The second approach will help you to focus on your effort and your progress, even when you have no external confirmation that you are progressing in the right direction. Focusing on your effort and personal progress will result in contentment and satisfaction throughout the semester, not simply relief at the end (see the figure that follows).

With this focus, your well-being will be linked to a process that is in your complete control (your effort) as opposed to an end result that is partially controlled by your professor (your grade). If you focus only on your end-of-semester grade (the uncertain conclusion), you are making a deal with yourself "to be unhappy until you get something."[8] In addition to increasing your life satisfaction and well-being, focusing your energy on what is in your control (your effort to learn the material) is also the most productive strategy to achieve the grade you desire. That is, focus on the journey, not the destination, as seemingly every grandparent likes to say.

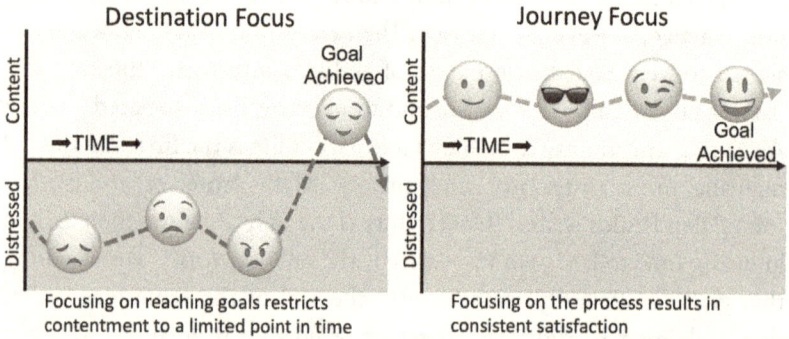

PRACTICE AND APPLICATION

There are two main categories of approaches that can be used to develop resilience in a world full of uncertainty. The first category focuses on bringing the *feelings* of discomfort associated with uncertainty into your consciousness where they can be questioned and analyzed rationally. Recognizing when your thoughts and feelings do not correspond with the reality of the situation will allow you to fix your disproportionate reactions and ensure that your actions will help you advance toward your goals. The second category of approaches will help you refocus your objectives so that the aspects of the course that are within your control become your only metric of success.

First, consider whether your anxious thoughts and feelings are appropriate. Defining the problem clearly and accurately is the first step in determining whether your thoughts and feelings are reasonable. In your notebook, describe how the uncertainty in your courses *actually* affects your life. Address only the direct effects resulting from grade uncertainty (i.e., lifting weights increases muscle mass) and avoid descriptions of emotional impacts (i.e., lifting weights makes me angry) or improbable secondary effects (i.e., lifting weights will increase my popularity).

It is likely that you found this question difficult to answer, and for good reason. Despite the fact that grade uncertainty can impact your emotions, it does not directly affect your grades, social status, or job prospects. I am able to identify only a few tangentially related effects, like not knowing if you are understanding the material in the way the professor intends. In light of the fact that grade uncertainty has few direct consequences on your present or future, consider the usefulness of your uncertainty-related anxiety. In your notebook, describe how your anxiety is beneficial or detrimental to attaining an external goal (i.e., earning the grade you desire, gaining recognition, becoming more popular, etc.).

Now describe how the anxiety is beneficial or detrimental to your well-being and life satisfaction.

You likely found that your anxious thoughts about grade uncertainty require considerable mental energy that could be used more productively. Use your notebook to determine if you can take any actions that would improve your educational experience despite grade uncertainty. For example, if you are uncertain that you are learning the material effectively, you can ask the professor or teaching assistant for general guidance, practice exams, study guides, or problem sets to assess your progress. Remember that asking for guidance about learning the material is always welcome (see chapter 10), whereas asking about your grade rarely is.

In many cases, there is nothing you can do about grade uncertainty that will improve your academic performance. There is little you can do if the course design makes the end-of-semester project worth half of the course grade, for example. Concerning yourself with this uncertainty will not aid your learning progress, it will cause discomfort, and it will take mental energy that could be used for studying or for worthwhile leisure activities. In cases like these, devoting mental energy to worrying about the uncertainty associated with the course design is not helpful at best and very harmful at worst.

In your notebook, write one to three brief statements that you can say to yourself to help you move your thoughts away from the anxiety-provoking uncertainty and toward meaningful, productive activities. Two that work well for me are "How useful are these thoughts to my education (or well-being)?" and "Will I care about this in six months?" The point is that if it will not matter to me in the near future, then it is not actually that significant (and it is not worth my time and effort now). The statements that resonate with you may be different from those that resonate with me. Furthermore, the statements that resonate with you will vary depending on the situation. Take a few moments to find statements that you could say to yourself that will help you to reduce your anxiety.

Contemplating your feelings and thoughts, describing them rationally and without emotional language, and evaluating how they affect your life can provide immediate, although temporary, relief from anxiety. The frequency and intensity of anxious thoughts and feelings will, however, decrease with consistent practice.

Although our society appears convinced that happiness results from achievements and awards, the rational basis underlying this conviction is misleading or outright wrong. Accomplishments take months or years of effort to achieve, whereas the moment of achievement occurs in a brief instant. Life satisfaction and well-being that is dependent on achievements means that you will be happy for only that brief instant, which is preceded and immediately followed by months of anxiety and dissatisfaction. Realigning your motivation from attaining accomplishments to achieving personal progress allows perpetual satisfaction and, ironically, will make it more likely that you will achieve the "accomplishments" society thinks are important (see the preceding figure). Realigning your motivation requires that you think rationally about the reasons you are attending college (see chapter 1) and the reasons you chose to take the courses you are taking.

In your notebook, briefly describe why you chose to take one of the courses that is causing you anxiety. Remember that "it is required to graduate" or "it looks good on my CV" suggests that the material in these courses does not interest you and that you should reevaluate why you are taking these courses (see chapters 1 and 12). In your notebook, describe what you would like to achieve by taking this course.

In your notebook, assess whether your goals for this course—what you would like to accomplish—are completely within your control. For instance, achievement-oriented goals such as "I want to know everything about marine biology" are not within your control, whereas process-oriented goals such as "I want to learn more about marine biology" are. Note that the first statement is centered on an outcome—"to know"—which is an endpoint that occurs in a single instance. The latter statement emphasizes your progress—"to learn more"—which is a process that is entirely dependent on your effort. By focusing your effort on goals that are within your complete control, you can achieve continual life satisfaction and academic success (see chapter 5). If your goals are not within your complete control—for example, worrying about how your exam responses will be graded—you are allowing others to determine when and if you experience relief from your anxiety.

In the following sections, you will design a plan to efficiently achieve goals within your complete control. This plan will focus on activities that maximize effectiveness and minimize costs. For example, you can increase your chances of learning and remembering material by seeking guidance on your study habits. This is relatively low cost but will have a significant impact on your educational progress. Keep in mind that progress is incremental and takes time.

In your notebook, outline a brief plan (bullet points) that prioritizes effort and progress in learning the material over exam scores. Among other things, this plan can outline a weekly study schedule, identify and correct grade-focused thought patterns, and address anxious thoughts and feelings before and during your studies. As an example plan that prioritizes learning, I recommend that students in my classes study for about thirty minutes every day, meet with a small study group every week, and use prior exams and problem sets as guides to ensure that they are learning the correct material. I also recommend that students explain what they have learned to their friends and family, especially to people with little background in the material, once every week or so. In addition to being internally rewarding, teaching others will allow you to recognize your fondness for the material, your progress, and the topics on which to focus your future study efforts. Because explaining the material clearly requires an in-depth understanding, teaching others provides a low-cost way to evaluate your current comprehension.

Remaining aware of your progress is essential to maintaining the motivation needed to consistently follow the plan you have just designed. Like many beneficial activities, this requires planning and intentional action. Similarly, children grow taller every week, but it is difficult to recognize this growth without regularly measuring their height (see chapter 14). In the absence of this action—measuring a child's growth or evaluating your educational progress—it would seem as if no progress has been made. By acknowledging your small wins every day, you will keep your effort and progress visible, which will keep you motivated. Every night, take five minutes to review your efforts and accomplishments that were aligned with your educational goals (i.e., progress in learning the material). Efforts or progress of any size deserve to be celebrated. This writing activity is similar to gratitude journaling, a technique widely recognized for promoting well-being and motivation.[9]

In your notebook, list three to four activities that you will engage in tomorrow that align with the plan you designed. Describe when and where you will perform or engage in these activities.

Congratulations! The plan you have designed to effectively attain your progress-oriented goals will reduce your anxiety by shifting your focus away from grade uncertainty and toward activities you can control. You should periodically evaluate and possibly alter your plan to remove activities that no longer serve their purpose and add activities that may be effective. As you learn and grow and as your courses change, your plan will need to be adjusted. Adapting your plan is evidence of progress, not a failure of the original plan.

PURSUIT OF THE GOOD LIFE

Many courses involve only a few highly significant evaluations, which can cause anxiety because students are uncertain about their final grades. Although this course design may seem unfair—and may actually be unfair—there is little students can do to change it. The ability to deal with this uncertainty in a calm and rational manner will improve your well-being throughout the semester and reduce anxiety that would otherwise take up brain power that could be used for learning. By contrast, if you indulge in the anxiety associated with grade uncertainty, you'll decrease your well-being and life satisfaction throughout the semester and reduce your ability to learn the material, thereby reducing your chances of earning high marks. A careful examination of the facts will reveal that worrying about your grade is not helpful and is often harmful. By focusing on your effort and progress—activities that are under your complete control—instead of grades, you will increase your well-being and, paradoxically, achieve higher grades. Importantly, altering your focus will allow you to achieve life satisfaction throughout the semester while working toward the high-quality goal of self-improvement—the definition of the pursuit of the good life.

KEY POINTS

- Course grades are heavily influenced by a few major end-of-semester exams or projects, leaving students uncertain about their expected grade throughout the semester.
- Anxiety associated with this uncertainty decreases your ability to achieve high marks as well as your well-being and life satisfaction. Accepting the uncertainty, by contrast, increases your well-being, academic performance, and grades.
- Attaining achievements takes time and effort, whereas the moment of achievement occurs in a brief instant. Well-being that is dependent on achievements means that you will be happy only for that brief moment when the achievement is attained, which is preceded and immediately followed by months of anxiety and dissatisfaction.

CHAPTER TWELVE

COURSE PLANNING

Kaila was pleased with her first semester courses and her plans for the second semester. She had enrolled in introductory courses in five different academic areas and has learned a lot about what she likes and also what she dislikes. As a result of her first semester courses, she was exposed to many novel scholarly topics, she fulfilled several general education requirements, and she now has a better idea of what majors would be a good fit for her. Before deciding which major to pursue, Kaila planned to spend her second semester exploring other potential directions and fulfilling additional general education requirements. She is now beginning to doubt if this is the best strategy. Several of her peers had already chosen their academic specializations before arriving on campus, and some will complete all foundational courses in their majors during their first year. Kaila has not even finished her first semester and she already feels like she has fallen behind. Her meeting with a counselor from the college advising office only served to make Kaila *more* anxious. During their meeting, the counselor explained his reasoning for why she is, in fact, falling behind and encouraged her to declare a major as soon as possible. He cautioned her that many of the courses she would take while "exploring" (he used finger quotes!) would not count toward her degree and would be a waste of time and resources. He explained that any delay in declaring a major would require her to take several difficult upper-level courses in her senior year and a long delay could result in the need to take summer courses or even stay an extra semester. Further, he mentioned that she may also lose the chance to spend a semester abroad, which she has been dreaming about since high school, if she fails to make progress on her major requirements. It feels like Kaila is being pushed to choose a major as soon as possible and, in a sense, her career path, all at age nineteen. At the same time, Kaila is tormented by the fear that she will choose the wrong major, dooming her to a miserable life with a career she finds intolerable.

> *Take time for all things: great haste makes great waste.*
> —BENJAMIN FRANKLIN[1]

It is common for students to feel pressured to complete their college experience as soon as possible. For students who are certain about their major and career path before enrolling, a focused and efficient path may even *seem* logical. Research[2] and my experience as an educator, adviser, and student, however, indicate that a narrowly focused route to graduation is rarely beneficial and is often detrimental for several reasons.

First, the idea that first-year college students should know exactly how they want to spend the next fifty years of their lives is absurd. Almost no college freshman has ever even heard of the majority of the possible academic subjects they could study (e.g., ecogastronomy?) or professions they could pursue (e.g., ethical hacker?). It is impossible for students to know if they are interested in areas if they do not know they exist. Even when students are aware that a profession exists, they likely have limited direct experience with the profession and even less theoretical knowledge. As an example, though all students are familiar with physicians, most (a) are unaware of the majority of careers in the medical field, (b) have never experienced the daily routine of a physician and cannot tell whether they would enjoy it as a career, and (c) do not know if they will enjoy studying the materials needed to become a physician. Through the study of both academic and practical foundations, which can be accomplished in college, you can accurately identify career paths that will be fulfilling and result in life satisfaction.

Second, many students change their minds after learning about new subjects in college (see Sara's story in chapter 1).[3] By exploring multiple subjects in your first year of college, you will be able to select the right major while limiting the time you spend on an academic path that you will not enjoy.[4] Even if a student takes an extra semester or two to declare a major, they can generally complete their degree requirements within four years. In fact, there are only twelve to sixteen courses required for most college majors, which can be completed in three to four semesters if necessary. A student who changes his or her major during senior year, however, will have difficulty avoiding summer school or additional college semesters.

Third, leaving college one or two semesters early has only one obvious benefit: tuition. Taking a heavy load of courses will prevent you from experiencing much of what college has to offer because your college experience will be cut short (see chapter 3). Moreover, you will not be able to take advantage of any of the opportunities and experiences that will occur after you graduate. Taken together, early graduation will deprive you of the experiences that most of us remember with great fondness just to be granted a degree six months early.[5] If tuition is not an insurmountable hurdle, graduating with your class will provide many positive benefits in the moment and in your future.

Many students feel constantly pressured by their parents and peers to unveil the blueprint of their future, which, if followed, will lead to "success" in life (see chapters 2, 9, and 16). It is assumed that selecting a major is the first step in the master plan that will guide you into your promising future. Students often believe that if they choose a major and progress rapidly toward completing their college career, which will move them closer to achieving this "success," they will be able to ease the pressure from their parents and peers. By choosing your path to "success" before you are confident that you will enjoy the area, you will, ironically, reduce your chances of being successful and will decrease your life satisfaction and well-being in the process.[6] Great thinkers throughout history agree that "Unreasonable haste is the direct road to error."[7] As examples, you are more likely to be uninterested in your courses, more likely to change majors, which may require you to take summer courses or stay extra semesters, more likely to require additional education after graduation in order to switch careers, and more likely to be dissatisfied with your career for the rest of your life, to name just a few. To summarize, it is very likely that you will regret deciding on a major and career you dislike simply to relieve parental or peer pressure. In contrast, you are unlikely to regret spending a few semesters finding the life path that is right for you (see chapter 1).

The primary message of this chapter is to encourage you to explore your options, identify your interests, and ignore the noise. To be clear, I am not encouraging you to spend all your time playing video games because you like video games—just the opposite, in fact. I am encouraging you to experience many topics and possible careers in order to identify those that will bring you a lifetime of fulfillment (playing video games is a fun distraction for most; by contrast, creating, coding, and testing video games are serious academic pursuits and careers that you may want to explore). College provides you with the perfect opportunity to gain both the theoretical and practical knowledge that will allow you to design the life plan that is most likely to be fulfilling. College can allow you to fulfill the aphorism "Find something you love to do and you'll never have to work a day in your life."[8] Rushing through college, by contrast, is counterproductive to the true mission of higher education (see chapter 1) and will hinder your ability to identify areas that can propel you toward success (without incredulous quotation marks).

As a final thought, the exploration of a wide range of subjects adds value to your life, regardless of whether you use the knowledge in your career.[9] Knowledge has intrinsic value, and there is no limit to how much you can learn in your lifetime (see the introduction to this book). General education courses are beneficial both as a means to identify areas of study you would like to pursue *and* as a means to become a more knowledgeable person. If you find a number of interesting and worthwhile subjects to pursue, you may feel anxious about picking the "wrong" major or career. However, if life satisfaction is the goal, then any of these paths you identify will likely allow you to attain it. Choose any one you think will bring you life satisfaction and you can safely move on without regretting your decision (see chapter 3).

PRACTICE AND APPLICATION

One of the most challenging aspects of exploring academic areas—which is essential to identifying a gratifying major and career path—is the pressure you may feel from your parents, advisers, and peers. The exercises in this chapter will help you to ignore those pressures and to focus exclusively on gaining the information necessary to make your best possible decision.

What Is the Worst That Can Happen?
Although most people advise us to think only of the positives, this exercise takes the opposite approach, and with proven results.[10] Leaving worst-case scenarios unexamined results in fear of an undefined and often exaggerated negative outcome. By contrast, confronting your imagined worst-case scenario will make it clear that the worst case is really not that bad and maybe not bad at all. In your notebook, explain what might happen if you ignore the pressure to choose an academic or career path immediately. For now, avoid internal dilemmas such as feeling anxious about falling behind your peers and concentrate instead on tangible consequences such as having to attend an extra semester.

Next, describe the possible consequences of choosing a career or academic path that you dislike. You are welcome to use those discussed in this chapter in addition to any others that come to mind.

Take a moment to compare the possible negative outcomes of delaying your decision to choose the best path for you with the possible negative outcomes of choosing a path toward a life you do not enjoy. Consider how these differing decisions will affect your life satisfaction and well-being in college and in your future career.

In nearly all cases, you will find that the disadvantages of spending an extra semester or two exploring your options are generally minimal, whereas the short- and long-term consequences of choosing a path you dislike can range from mildly troubling to catastrophic. For example, taking a few extra semesters to determine your optimal direction could cost you a few courses during one summer or even an extra semester to graduate. It is unlikely that you will pay this cost, however, as most college curricula have sufficient flexibility for students who take extra time to declare a major. Nevertheless, spending an extra four months in college is insignificant compared to advancing along an unsatisfactory path and living a less-than-satisfying life for the next fifty to eighty years.

The Grand Scheme of Things

Imagine your life fifteen years in the future. From the perspective of "future you," describe in your notebook how important it *has been* in your life that your college career lasted nine semesters as opposed to eight. Use the following prompts to guide your thinking: How has taking an extra semester impacted your life or career? How often do you discuss your total time spent in college, or even what your major was, fifteen years after you graduate? Will you or anyone else care about how many semesters you spent in college after you graduate?

Choosing a Major

Though this chapter focuses primarily on well-being and life satisfaction, a general set of guidelines can be helpful in choosing your major without the fear of missing out on the majors you will not choose (see also chapter 3). Although everyone uses a different process to make major decisions, there are some commonalities that can help you improve your decision-making capabilities (see chapter 1). In this section, you will use a major decision you recently made—deciding which college to attend—to illustrate the decision-making approaches shared by most people and to identify your unique style. You should start by explaining how you selected which colleges to apply to and why you selected the college you are currently attending. First, write the names of two colleges that you chose to apply to and two that you did not. The colleges that you chose not to apply to should be among those that you seriously considered (sorry, no Monster's University from *Monster's Inc.*). If you can remember, briefly describe in your notebook how you first heard about each of these colleges.

Next, describe any steps you took to determine which colleges you liked enough to submit an application (internet research, speaking with peers or a counselor, visiting the campuses, etc.).

Next, list two of your favorite colleges that sent you acceptance letters. I suggest that you focus on the two colleges that were most difficult for you to decide between. Briefly describe any actions you took to decide which college you would attend.

Now explore the following: Do you think your education, social life, or overall satisfaction would be substantially worse if you chose to attend the other college? If so, how? Consider the educational experiences, social life, and overall satisfaction of the students who attended this other college as you consider this question. Do you think they regret their choice?

You can discover many steps in the decision-making process by tracking your time line about which college to attend. In this instance, your decision-making process likely began when you heard about some colleges from family, counselors, or peers. After a cursory examination of each college, you likely narrowed your options to several colleges. Subsequently, you likely studied these colleges in greater detail, which increased your interest in some, decreased your interest in others, and possibly discovered other colleges that were of interest to you. You may have then visited one or several colleges to gain a better understanding of what life would be like if you attended these institutions. Only after gathering a great deal of information were you able to make a well-informed and rewarding decision. These exercises likely also revealed that you would have been equally successful and happy had you chosen the other college you regarded highly; your life would have been different, but you would still be successful.

Many of your future decisions, such as choosing your major or career path, will follow a similar pattern. That is, you will learn about courses and majors from advisers, parents, and peers; you will investigate each to determine which is right for you (and identify others through your investigation); you will take some introductory courses in these areas to gain practical knowledge; then you will choose among several paths that will lead to success and life satisfaction. It is important to keep in mind that there are many majors and careers that could bring you success and life satisfaction, not just one, just as there are many that would not be an ideal fit for you. Most people find that investigating and exploring through introductory courses is the best way to find out what direction is right for them.

To begin your exploration of potentially interesting directions, list five subject areas that you think could be interesting. Briefly describe the subject and why you might be interested in it in the left column. In the right column, identify one course offered at your institution that you could take to learn more about this area. I encourage you to further investigate these courses by talking with an adviser or peers and select one or two to take next semester. In the worst-case scenario, you will discover that there are many paths that would make you happy, which is an excellent position to be in.

TOPICS OF INTEREST	COURSES
Food equity, sustainability, pesticides, and genetically modified foods. I am interested in environmental and climate change.	ENVS 110: Ecogastronomy: The Art and Science of Food
Online security and personal information protection. I enjoy computer programming, problem solving, and helping make the world more fair.	ITM 480: Ethical Hacking

PURSUIT OF THE GOOD LIFE

The advantages of exploring academic fields and career options in order to determine your level of interest always outweigh the meager advantages of making a quick decision, in my experience. Accurately identifying and progressing in an enjoyable direction is the key to pursuing the good life. In addition, no one will care if you take summer courses or additional semesters to earn your degree after you graduate, tuition aside. By contrast, choosing a major or career path before you are certain that you will enjoy it always has more disadvantages than advantages. Although settling on a major immediately may temporarily ease parental and peer pressure, choosing an unsatisfactory path will lower your immediate sense of well-being and lead to long-term disappointment. Taking the time to gather the information you need to make the right decision can mean the difference between enjoying the rest of your life and living a dreary one. Take the time you need to choose wisely.

KEY POINTS

- Thoughtfully exploring multiple subject areas—an essential step to identifying a satisfying major and career path—can be frustrated by pressure from your parents, advisers, and peers.
- Quickly settling on a major may temporarily ease parental and peer pressure but could lead to an unsatisfactory academic and career trajectory that decreases immediate well-being and could cause long-term disappointment.
- Exploring a range of subjects will add value to your life, regardless of whether you use the knowledge in your future career.
- Explore your options, identify your interests, and ignore the noise.

CHAPTER THIRTEEN

THE AUTHENTIC LIFE

The summer before she started college, Clara was confident in her goals, abilities, and values. She was determined to become a lawyer, and she had no doubts about her core identity as a small-town girl who held strong, traditional values. Her first year at a large university located in a major metropolitan city led her to question her previously unwavering self-image as well as her life and career plans. During her freshman year she encountered novel ideas and philosophies, academic subjects and careers, and people from vastly different backgrounds; to call the experience "eye-opening" would be a huge understatement. Clara still adheres to many of her more traditional values, but her view of what constitutes a good or ethical life has expanded substantially. Her knowledge of career options has also expanded beyond becoming a lawyer, physician, or engineer, which were the only career options she was even aware of during high school. Her newfound knowledge has not, however, strengthened her confidence, her sense of competence, or her sense of belonging. In fact, the exact opposite is true. She is anxious about losing her college friend group if she reveals her updated, more open set of values. The anxiety she feels is exacerbated by fear that her expanded set of values will disappoint her family and friends back home. In parallel, she fears disappointing everyone who has supported her path to becoming a lawyer. Clara believes that if she tells everyone she plans to pursue a career in journalism, they will assume she has "failed" because the path to becoming a lawyer is just too hard for her. The most difficult aspect of her life is that she feels like a fraud every day. Her actions and words reflect her past values and ambitions, but not what she believes and wants today. She finds hiding her true identity exhausting, anxiety-provoking, and depressing. Clara desperately wants to reveal her true self but she is worried about the potential backlash from her friends and family.

> *This above all; to thine own self be true.*
> —WILLIAM SHAKESPEARE'S *HAMLET*[1]

The purpose of college is to improve yourself by expanding your breadth and depth of knowledge and developing your system of ethical beliefs (see chapter 2). The process of self-improvement incorporates both academic knowledge and nonacademic topics like cultural awareness, tolerance, and principles. By definition, self-improvement involves change.[2] It can be tempting, however, to maintain a static self-image. This is because many believe that any change is an indication of prior failure or that the only people who have ever changed are those who adapt their values in response to the situation and people involved (see chapter 2). When you believe your values and ambitions should never change, communicating improvements in your life is difficult. It is illogical to believe that your values and ambitions should never change.

I am not suggesting that you should not live by a set of values that are well-considered. You should. You can use your values as guiding principles to differentiate right from wrong and to determine the best course of action in any situation.[3] Nevertheless, your values continue to evolve as a result of your expanding knowledge and life experiences.[4] Changing your values or ambitions based on self-improvement and reflection indicates growth and commitment to living an authentic life. Modifying your values and goals is part of the self-improvement process, which is why you are going to college. Further, aligning your actions and plans with your current values and goals is the definition of living true to yourself. In fact, living authentically requires you to evaluate your values and ambitions regularly.

Living an authentic life occurs when your actions and words are compatible with your beliefs and values. Being authentic means being true to yourself rather than imitating what you think you should be. The great poet, philosopher, and abolitionist Ralph Waldo Emerson[5] made clear that "To be yourself in a world that is constantly trying to make you something else is the greatest accomplishment." Further, there is overwhelming evidence that being true to yourself reduces anxiety, enhances self-esteem, improves interpersonal relationships, increases motivation, and provides guiding principles during tough times.[6] In other words, it is essential to live a life that is consistent with your values and goals in order to pursue the good life.

MENTAL HEALTH

Living inauthentically has been linked to increased anxiety and depression.[7] Having a disconnect between your ethical beliefs and your behaviors leads to tension and a feeling of dishonesty, as if you are an actor playing a character instead of actually living your life. Living in a way that is not true to yourself or your values also creates a fear of being exposed as an imposter by your peers. The act of concealing your values and goals also lowers your self-esteem, job satisfaction, engagement, and commitment at work.

RELATIONSHIPS AND BELONGING

It is common for people to form lifelong friendships in college. Only by being true to yourself and your values and by demonstrating them with your actions and words can you develop meaningful relationships.[8] You are valued by others based on your values. It is possible that you will lose part of your social network by revealing an updated set of values or goals. But only by being open about your values and goals will you be able to form the genuine and lasting friendships that are important in life. You cannot establish meaningful connections with people who do not support your values. It is important to note that authentic connections are formed between people who respect each other's values, not necessarily those who hold an identical set of values. Choosing to conceal your values and ambitions so that you are accepted by your peers may earn you many temporary acquaintances, but temporary acquaintances do not facilitate feelings of belonging or acceptance (see chapter 4).[9]

As a result, when you act in ways that are inconsistent with your values, you will not be able to form meaningful relationships, and the casual relationships you do form will dissolve when difficult conditions arise.[10]

SELF-WORTH

People who hide their values and ambitions communicate to themselves that they are ashamed of themselves, resulting in guilt and anxiety.[11] Inauthentic actions also degrade your values and goals and nurture feelings of immorality.[12] Self-esteem and feelings of self-worth come from being honest about yourself, both in private and in public. Research consistently shows that people who behave authentically, in general or in specific instances, feel better about themselves and have a more positive outlook on life and their futures.[13]

GUIDING PRINCIPLES

By regularly reevaluating your values and ambitions and by living in accordance with those values and ambitions, you can build the guiding principles you need to make difficult decisions. That is, by comparing each possible course of action against your clearly defined values, you can simplify your decision-making process.[14] In addition, intentionally defining your values and ambitions will help you prepare for difficult situations by considering in advance how someone with your values would act.

Given the many benefits of living authentically, it may seem surprising that so many people choose actions that are not aligned with their values and ambitions. There are, in fact, both real and perceived costs associated with living authentically.[15] For example, living in accordance with your values takes time and effort. People who lead extraordinary lives constantly reevaluate their values and goals and strive to ensure that their actions reflect these values and goals. Taking the time to reevaluate your values and actions is emotionally challenging, but the rewards are well worth the effort.

There are also potential social costs associated with living authentically. Expressing values or ambitions that differ from those of your friends and family can result in tension and even the loss of part of your social circle. This is, however, a blessing in disguise, because your life will improve when you move on from friends who do not support the authentic you.[16] The fear associated with these potential social costs is often the driving force behind decisions people make about how to live their lives. In making social decisions, most people do not consider the many benefits of living authentically, which far outweigh the costs. The exercises outlined in the section that follows will help you examine your values and goals consciously. Furthermore, these exercises will assist you in weighing the costs and benefits of living according to those values and goals when making decisions about how to live your life.

PRACTICE AND APPLICATION

Living authentically requires you to intentionally examine (and reexamine) your values and goals, to identify thoughts that might hinder you from acting in accordance with your values and goals, to assess the validity of those thoughts, to anticipate difficult situations in which you may conform instead of living authentically, and to design premeditated plans to help you choose actions and behaviors that align with your values before encountering difficult situations. The exercises in this chapter will help you guide yourself toward living an authentic life.

Identify Your Values and Goals

Although most people are guided by both ambitions and values, few take the time to consciously examine them. When you examine your ambitions and values intentionally, you will be able to discard those you do not identify with and recognize those that cause tension in your life. Furthermore, regular reevaluations will allow you to recognize changes and improvements in your goals and values. Your goals and values should be continuously reevaluated throughout your life, since you should expect that goals and values will change as you gain knowledge and experience (see chapter 2). To begin, use your notebook to describe three to five things you most desire in your life. This will help you identify your most desired ambitions.

In your notebook, describe three to five character traits of one or more people whom you admire. Focus on the character traits rather than the people who exhibit those traits. This practice will help you identify your core values.

You may notice that what you most admire in others differs from what you most desire for yourself. Furthermore, you may find that you do not admire people who have some of the desires you described. What you admire in others is a better reflection of your core values than what you desire. With your desired and admired lists in hand, spend three minutes to consider the person you would like to be. If what you admire aligns more closely with your core values than what you desire, you should consider striving to make what you value into what you desire for yourself. Aspire to become a person whom you would admire by identifying your core values and aligning your actions with those values. By aligning your goals and your values, you will be closer to living your authentic life. Use your notebook to create a plan to turn each of the traits you admire into something you desire for yourself.

Example

A character trait I value: Honesty

Situation that could challenge my value: There are many students who cheat on exams, giving them an advantage. As a result, I am often tempted to cheat to avoid being at a competitive disadvantage.

I plan to: respect my values more than the possibility of scoring higher through dishonesty.

I will not: worry that other students may enjoy a short-term advantage. It is not worth the cost of acting dishonestly.

This exercise is not intended to be done only once. The characteristics you most admire will change as you gain more knowledge and experience. Living authentically does not mean enshrining your values in stone. Being yourself means respecting your values, which can be accomplished through rigorous assessment, and acting in accordance with those values in the present moment. Only by understanding and acting according to your current core values can you live authentically in the moment.

Perceived Costs

It is common for people to fear the potential social cost of revealing their authentic values and goals. This is especially true when revealing your updated values and goals to family or to established social groups. You may fear that other people will think less of you or reject you entirely if they discover that you are no longer the person they once thought you were. By contemplating these fears and how they relate to reality, you can distinguish imagined costs from actual costs. Conversely, ignoring or suppressing these fears makes them seem more catastrophic than they actually are. Generally, the actual social costs of living authentically are lower and much less likely to occur than most people believe. In your notebook, give a brief description of the worst scenario that could occur if your authentic values were revealed to your social group. In other words, what would be the worst possible outcome if you revealed your true values and goals? For example, some of your acquaintances may tell you that they do not like you or may exclude you from social gatherings.

Now describe the actual *impact* of this "worst-case scenario" on your life in your notebook. In what concrete way would this scenario actually affect your life? Try to include only factual impacts while avoiding descriptions of your emotions. For example, avoid describing how you would feel if you were excluded from some social events. Instead, place a greater emphasis on what you will miss if you are excluded from social events. Although emotions are an important part of life, they are almost never helpful when evaluating potential costs and benefits. To make a fair evaluation, describe both the costs *and* the benefits of this worst-case scenario. As an example of a potential benefit, the pressure and associated disadvantages of behaving inauthentically are alleviated when you are excluded from activities that do not align with your values.

The next step is to estimate the probability that this worst-case scenario will actually occur (e.g., 10%). If it is very unlikely to occur, which is the most likely outcome in most cases, it is not worth considering. Even if the worst-case scenario is possible, it is not the only possibility. In your notebook, describe the most likely outcome. In what ways would this outcome actually affect your life? In order to make a fair evaluation, describe both the costs *and* the benefits of this most likely scenario. You may want to consider all possible outcomes using space in your journal, not just the most likely ones.

Evaluate the probability that the "worst-case scenario" you originally feared might occur will actually happen now that you have considered other possible outcomes (e.g., 0.1%). In most cases, after considering other possibilities, the estimate of the probability of the worst-case scenario occurring decreases.

It is extremely unlikely that your worst-case scenario will occur in the overwhelming majority of cases. Further, the reality is that most often it would not actually be that catastrophic even if the worst-case scenario does occur. In fact, the benefits of living authentically always outweigh the costs in the long run and almost always outweigh the short-term costs. Your *fear* of an uncertain and unspecified outcome will likely be the most negative impact of the worst-case scenario. Living authentically, on the other hand, almost always yields very large benefits regardless of the outcome that actually occurs. A greater understanding of the true costs and benefits can make the decision to live authentically much easier.

In the event that you determine that the worst-case scenario is likely to occur and could have serious short-term consequences, I recommend working with a trained professional. For example, if your family is likely to disown you for living your authentic life, please consult a trained professional to limit the short-term effects and to maximize the long-term benefits of living authentically.

Make a Plan

Having a plan for living in accordance with your values will make the decision to live authentically easier in every situation. Using your notebook, identify one or two situations in which you might act in a way that is inconsistent with your current values or goals. As an example, some of your acquaintances might pressure you to party through the night, which may conflict with your goal of exercising in the morning. For each situation, outline a plan describing how you will live according to your values or goals despite opposing social pressures. If possible, describe how you would feel if you lived by your true beliefs and how you would feel if you did not.

Living authentically—living in accordance with your values—can be challenging. Social situations frequently present themselves in which following the crowd seems easier, at least in the short term, even when doing so conflicts with your values and goals. For instance, you may be tempted to attend a late-night party to avoid negative social interactions, even though you do not really want to go and it conflicts with your ambitions or values. It is helpful to have a plan for how you will react in general or in specific situations so that you will be able to react in a way that you admire and you will feel confident about your decision. Making decisions that align with your core values will always result in better outcomes in the long run, and the short-term costs are often less than you think. A commitment to authentic living is essential to well-being and life satisfaction.

PURSUIT OF THE GOOD LIFE

The good life cannot be attained passively or by chance. People who lead amazing lives do so by living according to their values. However, examining and reexamining the values and ambitions that are the foundation of their authentic selves requires time, effort, and emotional energy. Regular reevaluation is crucial, as your values and ambitions continue to change based on your ever-expanding breadth and depth of academic knowledge, cultural understanding, tolerance, and ethics. Although many people reflexively think that altering their values is an indication of prior failures, these changes are actually evidence of personal progress. "The good life is a process, not a state of being. It is a direction not a destination."[17] Authentic living also requires time, effort, and emotional energy to ensure that your behaviors consistently reflect your values, especially when faced with potential social costs. Nevertheless, the benefits of living authentically are well worth the effort. These benefits include self-improvement, academic success, and quality relationships, in addition to life satisfaction and well-being. Thus, the pursuit of the good life requires living authentically.

KEY POINTS

- Living authentically—being true to yourself rather than what others think you should be—occurs when your actions align with your beliefs and values.
- Authenticity reduces anxiety, enhances self-esteem, improves interpersonal relationships, increases motivation, and provides guiding principles during tough times.
- Living authentically includes changing your values or ambitions through careful reflection of novel academic knowledge, cultural awareness, tolerance, and values. By definition, self-improvement involves change.

CHAPTER FOURTEEN

UNINTERESTING COURSES

Jean-Nicholas is simply not motivated. During his first few semesters in college, he eagerly explored his options and prepared himself for a rewarding career and life. Jean-Nicholas was thrilled to discover a passion for architecture and he carefully planned his remaining college semesters around his new interest. After six college semesters, he still believes that becoming an architect would be a rewarding and enjoyable career. However, he is having difficulty finding the motivation to continue learning the necessary skills. The number of courses he must take, both in general education and as part of his major requirements, that seem tangential to his goal of becoming an architect is not helping. These courses often feel like a waste of time and energy to Jean-Nicholas. He thinks the courses are time consuming but are not helping him progress toward graduation nor toward becoming an architect. How could he possibly stay motivated to do well in his courses over the next three semesters when they seem pointless and graduation seems so far off? He managed to maintain some motivation last semester by focusing on the opportunity to relax over winter break, but he did not return to campus with a renewed sense of purpose. A part of him wishes he could fast forward through his college experience so that he can join the workforce, where he can finally allow himself to be happy.

> *Lost time is never found again.*
> —BENJAMIN FRANKLIN[1]

Most of us have wished that we could just fast forward through a painful or stressful event in our lives. For most pursuits, however, surrendering part of your limited time on earth in hopes of better times in the future is not a wise decision.[2] You will encounter uncomfortable and stressful situations in the future, just as you encounter uncomfortable and stressful events in college. In college, you can learn how to cope with challenges while maintaining your well-being, which will prepare you for the challenges of the future. It is nevertheless common for people to sacrifice their contentment and well-being in the present in the hope that such sacrifices will help them to attain a future achievement that will provide satisfaction and well-being. Unfortunately, people regularly move the happiness goalposts, so that future contentment and well-being are short-lived. Basically, we tell ourselves repeatedly that once "this" is over, we can begin to enjoy life (chapter 11). However, once "this" is over, we immediately pursue the next goal and repeat the oft-broken promise that once we achieve it, we will allow ourselves to be happy.

Long-term projects often follow a trajectory similar to Jean-Nicholas's journey to becoming an architect.[3] As a result of the constant and strenuous efforts that are involved in the middle section of the project, the excitement that characterized the beginning of the project begins to fade. The motivation to accomplish a goal can quickly diminish when repeated obstacles slow progress.[4] Obstacles abound in the long middle portion of most projects. A continuous stream of obstacles leads to emotional fatigue, which depletes self-control and motivation, making subsequent obstacles more difficult.[5] It is during this exhausting middle section of projects that the choices of students diverge. There are some students who quit or do only the minimum required to graduate. Even though these students may still believe that their original goals and plans are worthy pursuits, the work necessary to prepare them for their future seems too large to overcome. The number of unexpected obstacles often causes these students to become disillusioned. The cause of disillusionment may be a lack of understanding of how much work is required to achieve the goal, ignoring the benefits of working hard, or not assessing their progress on a daily basis.

Some students persist through the long middle section despite constant disillusionment, as Jean-Nicholas did.[6] It is common for these students to do well in their courses, earning decent or even good marks, but they are unhappy and unmotivated, and their long-term retention of the material is limited. Loathing every moment of effort toward your goal makes for a difficult and unsatisfying life. All the same, many students choose to find their academic experience nearly unbearable. It is not surprising that students who dislike college wish that this period of their lives would pass more quickly.[7] There is one obvious problem for students who persist despite disillusionment: their future will look much like their present. That is, you will always be in the middle of a project with difficulties and setbacks, regardless of where you are in your career. Approaching every project with the mindset of "I just need to get past this" will leave you wishing for a future after this project, then after the next project, then the next project, until your last days. With this mindset, it is only after every project is completed that you can finally allow yourself to enjoy life. Taking this approach to its logical conclusion, it suggests that you should try to rush past every day of your life, promising yourself that you will enjoy only the last few moments of your life. How is it beneficial to sacrifice nearly all of the only life you have just to enjoy a few brief seconds of happiness on your deathbed?

The strategy that results in the greatest success and the greatest life satisfaction is to enjoy each step of the process on your way to achieving your long-term goals.[8] Remember, "The whole future lies in uncertainty, live immediately."[9] Everyone agrees that enjoying life while achieving your goals is the best way to live; the question is how to acquire this mindset. It is important to emphasize that this does not mean changing your project or your goals; it means changing the way in which you approach both the long-term goal and each step on the way there. There are three underlying sub-strategies within this strategy: focus on your effort, regularly review and celebrate your effort, and regularly reexamine your long-term goals. These sub-strategies direct your energy toward what you can control (your effort), acknowledge your progress, and ensure that your goals align with your values (see also chapter 13), all of which enhance well-being and life satisfaction. Additionally, regularly evaluating your long-term goal helps you maintain motivation and recognize your progress toward that goal. Progress toward distant goals is often gradual, making it difficult to see how your daily efforts contribute to your long-term objectives.[10] This is similar to the phenomenon that children perceive their growth differently than others do. My grandparents were amazed at "just how much you've grown" after not seeing me for three months, though I did not notice my growth because it occurred in imperceptible increments each day. Taking the time to notice your progress—like measuring yourself against the wall each day—will reveal your progress and help to maintain your motivation.

PRACTICE AND APPLICATION

Progress toward a long-term goal is rarely as rapid as we expect it to be and often *much* slower than we desire. In addition, it can be difficult to notice your progress toward a goal when it requires a great deal of effort or time. The three interconnected approaches described in this section will help you stay motivated to achieve your long-term goals and, crucially, to enjoy your time while you do. As an important caveat, these approaches should not be misconstrued as encouraging excessive effort that leads to burnout. By contrast, these approaches are designed to encourage well-being through a sustainable (i.e., enjoyable) level of effort that will help you progress toward worthwhile goals and life satisfaction.

Focus on Effort

Similar to one of the approaches in chapter 11, this practice will help you to focus on the journey, not the destination. Each night this week, write two or three mini goals that you will accomplish this week, or better yet, tomorrow. There is a catch, however: it must be entirely within your control to achieve each of the goals. For example, earning all A marks this semester is not in your complete control (professors determine the grades), but studying for thirty minutes each day this week is in your complete control.

By linking your mini goals to your effort, you will be able to gain satisfaction and contentment from the work you put in each day, as opposed to just when you reach the end result. This will connect your life satisfaction and well-being to something that is in your complete control—your level of effort—and thus well-being and satisfaction are always within your reach.

In your notebook, describe briefly what is enjoyable about the efforts presented above. Importantly, do not describe how the *results* of the effort are enjoyable. Explain how the *activity* is enjoyable, regardless of the outcome that may result. For example, I enjoy the sense of control and freedom I experience when driving a car, regardless of the destination (i.e., result) of the journey. You may find this practice challenging, especially if you describe yourself as "goal oriented," but it can generate greater motivation, well-being, and satisfaction in your life. By identifying the enjoyable aspects of your mini goals, you are likely to continue to put in the necessary effort.

Celebrate Effort and Progress

Even the achievement of relatively large successes may not appear to move you closer to your long-term objectives. Consequently, you may feel demoralized that you are not getting closer to your goal despite your efforts and progress. This approach will encourage you to refocus on the progress you are making—which is inspiring—rather than the amount of work remaining—which can be disheartening. Each night, take a few minutes to describe your efforts and progress from that day. You can describe effort and progress on traditional goals, such as studying and learning, as well as effort and progress on habits that will improve your well-being, such as taking the time to acknowledge and celebrate your efforts.

Regardless of how much effort or progress you have made, take the time to celebrate your accomplishments. Celebrations can be anything from noticing an internal feeling of pride in your effort, to enjoying a piece of chocolate, to discussing your progress with your friends and family. Anything that promotes positive feelings about your effort and progress. Getting together with close friends each day to celebrate each other's daily efforts and progress is a great way to fuel your motivation while maintaining lasting social bonds (see chapter 4). You may recognize that this exercise is similar to gratitude journaling, with a focus on daily progress, from the modern mindfulness movement and positive psychology.

Another great way to track your own progress, to improve your learning and content knowledge, and to give back to others is to become a teaching assistant or tutor. It can be time-consuming and challenging to teach others, but many find it immensely rewarding. Moreover, it has been well documented that teaching is the fastest and most effective way to gain a deeper understanding of any subject.[11]

Make the Best of Tomorrow

The aim of this practice differs from that of focusing on your effort, despite appearing similar. The purpose of focusing on your effort is to connect your well-being with activities that are entirely within your control, whereas the purpose of this practice is to align your short- and long-term goals with your values. To begin, briefly describe your short-term goals for tomorrow each evening (or morning, if you prefer) in your notebook. The following questions should be addressed in your daily goals:

- Is there something that can make *tomorrow* great? By asking this question, you will focus on the activity at hand rather than what could be achieved by your efforts.
- Are my short-term goals aligned with my long-term goals and priorities (see chapter 2)? Ensuring that your actions and goals align with your values (see chapter 13) is always a good idea to ensure that you have not veered off course.
- Are my mini goals the most effective way to achieve my long-term goals? Can I achieve my mini goals by taking actions that promote my well-being and life satisfaction? The journey can take many different paths, and some of them are easier than others. Choose the most efficient path to achieve your worthwhile goal, rather than the path of least resistance. Whatever the path you choose, ensure that you will enjoy well-being and satisfaction along the way.

PURSUIT OF THE GOOD LIFE

Why should you hate your time in college? If you plan to complete your degree requirements anyway and in a subject that you enjoy (see chapter 12), why not enjoy the process while doing it? The approaches in this chapter are designed to help you achieve success in your studies while maintaining a positive state of mind, a key feature in your pursuit of the good life. These practices are based on the premise that you will always get exactly what you want if you have complete control over the outcome of your efforts. If you associate success with the amount of effort you put into a worthwhile goal, you can never fail. That is, if you define "success" as giving your best effort, you will always succeed (and you will have a better chance of achieving high marks in your courses). Attaining your long-term academic or career objectives—which are not entirely under your control—is a rewarding byproduct of successful effort but should not be the measure of success. With this perspective, you can never be dissatisfied with the *outcomes* of your efforts, which are often out of your control, but you can always find satisfaction if you give your best *effort*. At times, the results of your efforts, such as the amount of progress toward your long-term goal, may be slow, but your well-being and life satisfaction should not be determined by these types of achievements. Research supports the interesting finding that if you enjoy your efforts during the journey, you are more likely to succeed and make fewer mistakes on the way.[12] You may not care that you are progressing more quickly if you are having a good time, but it is an advantage nonetheless.

KEY POINTS

- The unending stream of challenging or uninteresting courses can lead to emotional fatigue and reduced motivation. Many students persist through these courses, earning decent marks, but are unhappy and wish they could just get past this part of their life.
- The "I just need to get past this" mindset causes you to wish for your future after this course, then after the next course, then after college, then after retirement, until your final days; do not surrender any of your finite time on earth in hopes of a better future.
- Enjoying each step on your way to achieving your long-term goals will result in the greatest success and life satisfaction.
- To enjoy the process, focus on your effort, acknowledge your progress, and ensure that your goals align with your values; each enhances well-being and life satisfaction.

CHAPTER FIFTEEN

DEEP PROJECTS

Dillon has worked hard to accumulate an extraordinarily long list of accomplishments. He regularly compared this list of accomplishments to those of his classmates and was almost always reassured that his list was more impressive. During his last seven college semesters, he has shadowed a physician for two weeks, completed a three-week internship at an investment bank, volunteered for one month at a rehab clinic and for another week at a Wall Street think tank, participated for a few weeks as a student researcher in three different labs in two different departments, has been a member of four student clubs and was the treasurer of one of them for one semester, and has published an article in his college newspaper. The *number* of activities that Dillon could list on his résumé was greater than almost any of his peers. This sense of comparative superiority was a major source of pride and optimism about his future. In light of his remarkably long list of activities, Dillon cannot understand why all his professors and advisers have declined to write him letters of recommendation. Not a single mentor with whom he has worked is willing to write a letter on his behalf. Although most did not explain their reasoning, two professors did clarify that they did not have enough information to write a substantive letter about him. Professors thought he had not worked with their groups for enough time to accurately evaluate his potential. In addition, they said Dillon had not spent enough time participating in the project to determine whether this was an area he would enjoy pursuing. Dillon now recognizes that these experiences were not substantial enough to help him to clarify his interests. Consequently, he has no direction for his life after graduation and has not identified any subject areas about which he is passionate.

He is currently preparing applications to a wide variety of programs including medical schools, law schools, and internships in finance and politics. Despite his excessively long résumé, Dillon is concerned that he will not be accepted to any of these programs without substantive letters of support.

> *It is quality rather than quantity that matters.*
> —SENECA[1] (AND ALSO MY GRANDMOTHER)

The behavior of Dillon illustrates a very common pattern among college students—engaging in extracurricular activities solely to accrue a long list of "accomplishments" with which to impress others.[2] Many students briefly participate in several projects in order to boast about how many activities they have completed. They rarely consider the *quality* of their experiences, as they often assume that the number of activities is the measure of "success." These brief experiences, however, add nothing positive to their college experience, personal growth, social or professional network, life satisfaction, well-being, or career prospects, aside from an additional line to their future résumés.[3] These activities are akin to reading the summary of one random episode from multiple television series. Although you may know the general contours of each show and can participate in superficial discussions with the information you gleaned from the summaries, you do not understand the shows nor even whether you would enjoy watching them. You may not even be able to use these summaries to identify what kinds of shows would be of interest to you. Participating *only* in short-term activities in college has similar benefits, or lack thereof. That is, you will not gain an understanding of the topic nor what careers in that area might entail; you will not know if you would find a career in that area interesting nor will you know what types of careers could be of interest to you in the future; and the experiences themselves are unlikely to be fulfilling.

Students exclusively engage in short-term activities because they are told—implicitly and explicitly—that participating in more activities showcases their importance to peers, professors, awards committees, and future employers.[4] Students are told that validation from others, as well as how they should view their own success (see chapter 2), is based on the quantity, not quality, of their experiences. The misguided belief that a person's value is linked to the number of activities they participate in can be found (a) in the advice from many high school counselors who stress that colleges value students with many extracurricular activities, (b) in comparisons among peers who rank other students according to the number of their accomplishments, and even (c) in tepid praise from college professors who offer "Wow! You have done so much" after a cursory reading of a résumé.

It is an open secret that no one who is evaluating candidates for awards, internships, or jobs is deceived by the *length* of a résumé.[5] It is easy to recognize that students who participated briefly in many activities did so only to add another activity to their list of accomplishments. As an example, it is apparent that a three-week ride-along with an EMT does not indicate that a student has the capacity or discipline needed to practice medicine, the perseverance required for medical training, an understanding of what a medical career consists of, or even if the student would enjoy a career in medicine. Despite what high school counselors and your peer interactions suggest, students focused on adding accomplishments to their future résumés rarely find success with the committees that decide who is accepted to graduate programs or are involved in the hiring process[6]; these committee members are unimpressed by overly inflated résumés. These résumé-building students are aiming for recognition that they rarely receive when their résumés are evaluated.

Applause without self-improvement is contrary to the purpose of college and a hindrance to your pursuit of the good life (see chapter 1 and my definition of "the good life"). It is most effective and most enjoyable to spend your college years building academic and practical knowledge, learning resilience to adversity, and participating in activities to determine what you would enjoy doing after college.[7] Participating in longer duration (two to four semesters), deep, multifaceted projects that expose you to what a life dedicated to an academic or professional area would be like is the best way to make the most of your college experience. These types of extended projects are essential to identifying and cultivating your passions. Like anything of value, these projects will take dedicated effort and time. The great American Olympian Jesse Owens said of his own accomplishments, "in order to make dreams come into reality, it takes an awful lot of determination, dedication, self-discipline, and effort."[8]

Identifying the projects in which to invest your time and effort can be unnerving. Due to fear of making the wrong decision and wasting opportunities, many students either avoid working on any projects or switch to other opportunities whenever they hear of another one that interests them (see chapter 3). As outlined in the exercises that follow, one method for identifying projects in which you might be passionate is to engage in several on a short-term basis, either simultaneously or sequentially. When something is not right for you, you can often recognize it quickly and move on. Short-term experiences with unsatisfactory projects provide the equally valuable opportunity to learn what you do not enjoy. The purpose of this approach is to meet the primary objectives of college and to allow you sufficient time to look for the projects that will be most rewarding for you.

The importance of deep, multifaceted projects for your personal development and as preparation for your future career cannot be overstated.[9] Projects of this type facilitate the development of a variety of skills that are not readily available in courses including strategic, creative, and critical thinking, problem solving and analysis, learning to apply multiple perspectives and approaches, and effective communication and teamwork.[10] Focusing only on coursework may provide students with a strong conceptual foundation, but it does not provide them with the applicable and practical knowledge necessary to succeed in their future careers. By contrast, the experience and skills that make up the basis of most careers are acquired and demonstrated by students who also engage in extensive projects.[11] Additionally, these projects provide students the opportunity to explore areas of potential personal interest and to gauge their motivation and passion for the field. Lastly, long-term projects strengthen a sense of social and ethical responsibility by both applying knowledge across disciplines and by working in interdisciplinary teams. The exercises in this chapter will guide you through when and how to look for deep and multidimensional project opportunities. Additionally, they will help you evaluate your experience to determine if and when you should move on to another position.

PRACTICE AND APPLICATION

There are myriad reasons for you to engage in deep, long-term projects while in college, several of which are outlined in this chapter. These types of projects allow you to apply your classroom knowledge to practical, real-world problems as well as to take initiative, work effectively with people from diverse disciplinary backgrounds, and learn more about a specific topic. These projects will also allow you to demonstrate your newly developed skills to a professor or mentor who will then have the necessary information about you to write a strong letter of recommendation. You will still benefit from this letter even if it supports your application to a field that differs from your current project since the skills you will learn are universally respected. A major hurdle many students face is just getting started: how and when to search for these opportunities and how to obtain a position once you have found something interesting. How to determine if you should move on to a new opportunity often goes unasked. The exercises that follow address these two major aspects of engaging in an important part of your education and personal growth.

Finding Your Opportunities

Your experiences in and out of the classroom have helped you to identify an inspiring major and, hopefully, several career possibilities that may interest you. In order to determine whether you are passionate about working in these areas and not just reading about them in class, you need to devote some effort to a few directions of potential interest. You should evaluate each opportunity for its potential for personal growth, not only as a way to prepare for a future career, nor as a way to look impressive. By engaging in these activities, you will gain the experience you need to guide your future decisions.

As you begin this phase of your education, keep in mind that there will be many opportunities that could enhance your self-development and provide the information necessary for making informed decisions about your future. Every opportunity offers a unique set of benefits that can be appreciated only by experiencing them firsthand. Though choosing the "best" opportunity may initially cause some anxiety, the reality is much more reassuring. In truth, participating in a long-term project is important, but none of the opportunities you are interested in is inherently better than any others. Your future career path is not determined by the opportunities you participate in during college. In fact, very few people pursue a lifelong career in the exact area of their long-term undergraduate project. You can gain practical knowledge and skills from long-term projects, however, and use them to guide your future decisions.

Where to begin? The first step is to clearly identify your current interests. These should not be the interests of your parents nor interests that you think will make you look impressive to your peers (see chapters 2 and 9). In your notebook, list three to five academic or career areas that interest you. For each, use the knowledge from your coursework, extracurricular activities, and other experiences, as well as discussion with peers, to clarify why these directions are of interest to you. Your goal should be to identify directions that are inherently interesting to you, that you believe will provide life satisfaction. For now, avoid describing directions that are interesting because they will provide the highest monetary return; we will incorporate these ideas in a moment.

Do not be discouraged if it takes several attempts to clarify your thoughts about the areas you find most interesting; this is expected. Put this exercise aside if the interests you have identified do not resonate with you or are ambiguous and rework it in a few days.

Using your clearly delineated interests as a guide, identify professors from your prior coursework that teach subjects related to your areas of interest. These professors can provide you with information about ongoing projects in their field in which you may be able to participate. In most cases, your professors will facilitate an introduction between you and a colleague with whom you might work, since guiding students to success is one of the most satisfying aspects of our jobs. Importantly, you should *not* contact only one professor or focus on only one area of interest or one project at this point. I suggest treating this stage like speed dating; use it as a way to gain a little experience before deciding on a longer-term commitment.

In your notebook, write a short and direct email to a professor explaining that you want to participate in a long-term project, why you are interested in a long-term project, your current situation, and your future plans. In the example below, I have provided a sample email that might be useful to a student looking to get involved in scientific research, which is my area of study. The text can be modified to fit your interests or written in your own style.

> Dear Professor Brisson,
>
> I have enjoyed my biology courses and would like to continue my education by participating in a scientific research project. I am considering a career as a research scientist, and I believe that participating in the scientific process will help me decide whether this is the right path for me. I am writing to ask for your advice and if you can facilitate a meeting with some of your colleagues. Although my main goal is to gain research experience and contribute to scientific discovery, I am particularly interested in the research conducted in the labs of Professors Metcalf, Ding, and Graham. Ideally, I would volunteer in a few labs for about three weeks (five to ten hours per week) to identify the most appropriate opportunity for me. My goal is to obtain a deep, multifaceted experience in one lab by engaging in an ongoing research project for at least one year, either as an independent study or as a student research assistant.

The sample email includes several essential elements: (a) it demonstrates that you are focused on an important part of your education—practical experience and deeper learning—and that you have a functional plan; (b) the specifics of your plans are flexible and motivated by a desire for self-improvement through experience; (c) your request is specific; and (d) you are allowing your professor's colleagues to evaluate you and your dedication prior to them committing to any long-term support. The email you write will be better received if it contains these elements. If you are pursuing options in different disciplines or if your interests change, you may need to send multiple emails with these elements.

Do not be discouraged if your professors do not reply immediately or do not reply at all. Professors receive hundreds of emails each day and important messages can be lost or forgotten. Some professors may not reply to your first email to test your dedication, assuming that students who are truly interested will send a follow-up email. If you do not receive a response after a week, send the same email again to push your message back to the top of their inbox. I suggest sending the same email once per week for about five weeks. If you do not receive a response after five or six messages, it is unlikely that this professor will be helpful. It is important that you do not take this as a personal rejection; there is almost no chance that the lack of a response has anything to do with you in particular.

Regularly Evaluate Your Experience

It is important to evaluate your experience regularly once you have committed to a long-term project. Regularly evaluating your experiences, especially in writing, will guide your decision-making both while in college and in the future. Assess your experience once or twice per month in your notebook by addressing the following prompts: What do I enjoy about my project and why? Which parts of the project are less enjoyable and why? What have I learned (or how have I improved) through this project? For these questions, focus on what is enjoyable about your experience right now. Avoid "necessary evil" sentiments such as "I do not enjoy this experience but it will be helpful for me in the future." You will reflect on how the experience affects your future in the following exercise.

Next, evaluate your future career options on the same bimonthly basis by answering the following questions: Am I still passionate about this path? Is this the type of work I would enjoy in my career? It is important to incorporate your answers above into your thinking about these questions, but also to keep them in the proper perspective. For example, you may like your current colleagues (enjoyable now), but that does not guarantee that all your future colleagues in this field will be equally congenial. Similarly, although you might find writing editorials for your school newspaper unsatisfying, that does not mean that you will not enjoy investigative reporting or writing novels. On the other hand, if you dislike the scientific process—which permeates all science-based careers—then a career in scientific research may not be for you.

These evaluations can be used both to determine if you should find a new long-term project as well as to determine the careers that are most likely to result in life satisfaction. If you evaluate the disappointing aspects of projects rationally, the majority of them are not substantial enough to motivate you to switch projects. Taking the time to rationally assess the entirety of the experience with respect to your immediate goals (self-improvement, personal growth, and knowledge for future decision making) will help you to get the most from the experience, to learn from the disappointing and inspiring aspects, and to prevent you from abandoning a quality experience due to emotional reactions to real but manageable setbacks.

PURSUIT OF THE GOOD LIFE

Traditional college courses provide the foundational information necessary for the study of any subject, but they are not the only educational aspect of your college experience. The purpose of courses, even highly specialized courses, is to impart a breadth of knowledge from an established canon. Learning through courses is essential, but it cannot deliver a focused, in-depth understanding of a specialized subject, practical application and skills, experiential knowledge, nor an understanding of the methods used to discover new knowledge. Moreover, reading about a topic rarely supplies the necessary information to determine whether careers in the field are likely to be satisfying. Long-term projects provide you with practical knowledge, technical capabilities, problem-solving skills, and hands-on experience in an area in which you might be interested in pursuing a career. These projects also provide a professor or mentor with sufficient information to write a strong letter of recommendation on your behalf. Additionally, long-term projects build universally respected skills such as strategic and critical thinking, problem solving and analysis, and communication and teamwork, none of which coursework is designed to teach. The knowledge you gain from coursework often serves as the basis for long-term projects, which advance your understanding beyond what you would gain from coursework alone. Many students find their long-term projects to be their most enjoyable learning experiences. They are also where students learn the most about a particular topic and about themselves. A long-term project is an ideal way to cultivate your rational faculties while enjoying a positive state of mind—an ideal way to pursue the good life.

KEY POINTS

- Long-term, multifaceted projects facilitate the development of many skills that are not taught in most courses but that are essential for your personal development and as preparation for your future career.
- Short-term experiences provide opportunities to learn what you do not enjoy, but students who briefly participate in many short-term projects to impress others are aiming for recognition they rarely receive.
- Committees evaluating candidates for awards, internships, or jobs are rarely deceived by the *length* of a résumé; they easily recognize that these students want validation based on the quantity, not quality, of their experiences.

CHAPTER SIXTEEN

AFTER COLLEGE?

As Ashna nears graduation, she is proud of the academic and personal growth she has achieved. There is no doubt that her first two semesters were challenging. Without the structure her parents had imposed on her in high school, as well as the social insecurities that often arise in new college students, Ashna spent much of her first year socializing every night and anxiously avoiding coursework. Given her effort, the grades she earned those semesters are exactly what anyone would expect. Through an incredible demonstration of resilience, willpower, and determination, Ashna was able to refocus her remaining six semesters on learning and a more constructive social life. Her pride in the grit, effort, and dedication to improving herself that she had demonstrated—values that now represent her core identity—was shattered during a weekend trip home to celebrate her grandmother's birthday. Her family members often began conversations by congratulating her on her upcoming graduation, but they never missed an opportunity to ask what she would do *after* graduation. Her response to this question—that she won a competitive internship that would allow her to explore modern media marketing as a potential career—was met with skepticism from some and outright criticism from others. These encounters left Ashna feeling as if her accomplishments during college and in obtaining this prestigious, albeit transitional, position were trivial and not worth celebrating. Similar to how she felt during her first semesters of college, Ashna began to feel that she was already behind in the next stage of her life, which caused her anxiety to escalate and her self-esteem to crumble. Ashna is eager to share her joy with her family, but they are already concerned about the next set of obstacles she will face. Ashna felt unsupported, alone, and deflated as she made her way back to campus.

> *No one does wrong voluntarily.*
> —SOCRATES[1]

Almost everyone faces unrelenting questions from their family about their future plans. Although these questions can be disheartening and can quickly become annoying, they are rarely malicious. In nearly all cases, your family is genuinely concerned about your happiness and success. Nevertheless, they are concerned about your future, just as you are, and are worried about any uncertainties in your plans.[2] Further, your family has no control over your plans and your actions. As we have discussed throughout this book, the absence of a sense of control is a major source of anxiety for everyone. Your family pressures you for concrete answers because they want to be reassured that you will always be happy and successful. Although appreciating the motivations of your family may eliminate the annoyance of these interactions, it is unlikely to immediately eliminate the anxiety that these interactions can cause.

Critical questions about your future plans, from your family or from others, can cause anxiety for at least three reasons. First, completing your college degree is a significant milestone that requires an enormous and sustained effort, an effort that deserves to be recognized and celebrated.[3] If you are asked a judgmental question about your next steps, it might give the impression that your accomplishments in college were trivial, only a minor obstacle that anyone can overcome. Second, such questions often confirm our own self-doubt. When people are going through a major transition, such as finishing a multiyear degree, they are especially susceptible to both excitement and anxiety.[4] Having to answer these critical questions validates our own nervous thoughts about our next steps, which further exacerbates our anxiety. Third, these questions are often presented as judgments or criticisms. When asked these kinds of questions, we feel as if we have disappointed our family when we expected them to celebrate a crowning achievement with us.

It is important to reiterate that these questions may be clumsy and ineffective but are not meant to be hurtful. Your family is proud of you and your accomplishments, even if they do not know how to show it. The fourteenth Dalai Lama advises, "Do not let the behavior of others destroy your inner peace."[5] Their fears during this time of transition and uncertainty in your life, and in their lives, are powerful motivators of their actions. In fact, they are probably not aware that their words can negatively affect you or realize that their questions do not even provide them any reassurance. By knowing they come from a place of caring rather than criticism, these tactless questions become harmless and possibly even endearing. Remember that your family and friends do not do wrong on purpose.[6] They are doing the best they can given their current level of anxiety. If you can understand and forgive their misguided actions, you will increase your own well-being and self-confidence, their well-being and their confidence in your future plans, and your probability of career success. I agree that it is unfair to burden you with the responsibility of interpreting difficult comments from your family in a more positive light, as opposed to burdening them with behaving more appropriately. However, taking responsibility for what you can control—your own actions—is almost always the best option for increasing your well-being during your pursuit of the good life.

Soon-to-be college graduates as well as their friends and family experience anxiety and insecurity during uncertain times.[7] Repeated questions about your future can exacerbate your anxiety about one of the most uncertain life transitions you will experience. It is likely that much of your life had a predetermined plan with many safeguards, but the choices you make now are nearly unbounded and without any obvious protections against failure. Cross-examinations by your family and friends can validate your self-doubts and increase your anxiety. Remember that experiencing some uncertainty about your future is both normal and acceptable. Also know that you have ample time to find your ideal path, and that your education provides an effective safety net.

It is simply unnecessary to have a detailed road map for your future when you finish college. In spite of pressure from others, taking time to explore potential paths can often be beneficial and is sometimes necessary. It is common for both very successful people (such as Supreme

Court Justice Ruth Bader Ginsburg[8]) and moderately successful people (such as me and many of my colleagues) to explore the vast collection of possibilities after graduation before settling on a more permanent career path. If you decide it would be worthwhile for you to explore your possibilities for a year or more, make sure you do explore your possibilities; do not waste time doing nothing. The experiences you gain during these years of exploration can guide you toward a rewarding career only if you use them to discover your options. During this period of exploration and self-discovery, you will discover what interests you and what does not, as well as gain valuable experiences that will enrich your life and prepare you for a fulfilling future.

It is important to note that I am not suggesting that you should not make money during this time—you need to pay for food and housing and other necessities. I am suggesting that making money should not be your only objective. It is possible to eat and find your ideal career path by exploring your possible future paths through jobs and internships that can clarify your interests and allow you to continue your self-improvement journey.[9] Never forget that "Not all those who wander are lost."[10]

Many students are afraid of disappointing their family and friends if they do not immediately pursue the career that logically follows their degree.[11] It is true, however, that many people have been extremely successful *because* they did not choose the traditional career path based on their college degree. For example, the Nobel laureate in Physiology and Medicine (1989) and former director of the National Institute of Health, Harold Varmus, was an English major before attending medical school.[12] In fact, almost three quarters of all college graduates pursue careers that are completely unrelated to their college degrees.[13] Although many careers require a bachelor's degree, more than 90 percent of employers believe critical thinking, problem-solving, and communication skills are more valuable than the collegiate major of prospective candidates.[14] Innovation is often necessary to address the complexities and interdisciplinary nature of modern careers. Even Silicon Valley frequently favors candidates with a broad liberal arts background or with experience in fields other than software engineering because innovation often comes from broadly educated people with diverse backgrounds. As these data demonstrate, you will benefit from your college education even if your career path does not follow the common expectations for those with your major.

PRACTICE AND APPLICATION

College graduation is a time of transition and uncertainty for every student. This applies both to you and to your family. The anxiety associated with this time of transition and uncertainty can lead to counterproductive behaviors from family members who do not decrease the uncertainty and often cause more anxiety. The following approaches are designed to help you recognize your anxious thoughts and ensure that they are appropriate given the circumstances. The first set of approaches focuses on your own self-doubt, and the second set focuses on dealing virtuously with loved ones who fail to express themselves constructively.

Question Judgments about Yourself

I would like to congratulate you on your achievements both inside and outside of the classroom during your time in college. Seriously, it is a great accomplishment in which you should take pride. It is easy, however, to undervalue these accomplishments. You see people every day who have bachelor's degrees (or will soon), which can make graduating from college seem like a trivial obstacle that anyone can easily overcome. It is not. Only 36 percent of Americans older than twenty-five have earned a bachelor's degree, putting you in an elite group of highly accomplished individuals.[15]

In your notebook, provide a realistic and comprehensive description of your accomplishments. In your description, focus on how you have grown as a person and scholar without mentioning how it will impact your future. That is, personal and academic growth is progress that should be celebrated on its own merit, not only as a stepping stone to a career. What you do next with your education does not affect the remarkable success of your educational experience. Take pride in what you have accomplished; it is significant.

Next, describe how your college experience has enriched your life. A good strategy is to compare your current life with what you might have had if you had not graduated from college. What would you be doing now if you had not attended college? What would your life look like?

It is also helpful to put your thoughts concerning the uncertainty about your future into a broader context. Even though logic suggests that not identifying your ideal trajectory until after you graduate could have many advantages and no disadvantages, the discomfort caused by this uncertainty can result in an emotional response that replaces rational thinking. Consider both the positive and negative consequences of being uncertain about your future in your notebook. Begin by briefly writing two or three possible directions you might explore over the next two years. Do you feel like you would be happy with a career in each of these possible directions?

Several of the directions you described, as well as many other possibilities, are more likely than not to lead to a fulfilling career. As you can see from your analyses, there are many options available to you, and most will result in life satisfaction if you allow them to! Given the number of good options available, you have little cause for worry.

Next, use your notebook to explore why it is worrying not to know precisely what your future holds. Try to identify the exact cause of your anxious thoughts. Include an assessment of (a) the likelihood that the outcome you are anxious about will actually occur and (b) why this outcome is actually "bad"—how it negatively impacts your life in real terms. As an example, you might worry about your career lagging one year behind your classmates, which is possible, although most of your classmates will change jobs several times before settling on a more permanent career. I cannot think of a single reason why this is "bad" for you.

Use your notebook to describe the advantages and disadvantages of taking the time needed to explore your options if it will help you choose the most suitable career. Compare these to the advantages and disadvantages of choosing a direction now that is not right for you.

Question the Judgment of Others

The desire to feel respected and valued is a human instinct that likely evolved in our hunter-gatherer ancestors (see chapter 9). Further, it is especially important for us to feel respected and valued when dealing with our family and close friends, the very people who often criticize and ask uncomfortable questions. Your emotional reaction to critical, probing questions from your family and friends can make you feel less respected and less valued, but this is unlikely the intent of the questions.

Despite their indelicate words or actions, your family and close friends genuinely care about your success and happiness. If you understand what they are trying to say, their words will be less damaging, and your relationships will be strengthened as a result. What questions have you heard or expect to hear about your postgraduation plans? Please write them in your notebook.

For each of these questions and what you know about the questioner, try to infer their intent using your notebook. That is, determine what your family members or friends are *trying* to accomplish by asking you these questions. Remember that no one does wrong on purpose and those who care about you are very unlikely to want to hurt you.

Although you may know that your family and friends wish you happiness and success, they are also anxious and may be concerned that your plans, or lack thereof, could derail your future. People who care about you are affected by this period of transition and uncertainty in the same way that you are affected by it. Recall one time (or many, in my case) when you have made impolite comments to those you care about, despite supportive intentions. In a similar way, the anxiety generated by this period of uncertainty can result in insensitive comments and questions from family and friends. Understanding their intentions can neutralize the negative effects of their words on your well-being.

To help yourself internalize the intentions of your undiplomatic family members, compose a brief note of appreciation for the support and care they *intend*, regardless of their actual words, in your notebook. Before you begin writing your notes of appreciation, take a moment to sympathize with their anxiety, or even empathize, as you may also have worries about your uncertain future. In your notebook, write an individualized note of appreciation to each person with good intentions but less-than-perfect behavior. These notes should not contain any negative comments about the unsatisfactory actions of those who support you. Concentrate only on their positive intentions in your notes to them.

Take a moment and consider the actual impact of these annoying questions. In other words, how do these questions negatively affect your life? You may prefer kind words to criticism, but neither directly affects your life (see chapter 2). You cannot be harmed by words unless you let yourself be harmed; you have heard the proverb, "sticks and stones. . . ."

It is not what others do or say that impacts your life, but how you react to what they do or say. Allowing yourself to be upset by their words causes infinitely more harm than the words or actions themselves. In your notebook, describe how the comments you have heard or expect to hear impact (or do not impact) your life *if* you do not allow them to upset you. Is your future trajectory more or less uncertain as a result of these comments? Are they going to prevent you from graduating? Will they make you less attractive to employers (or potential partners)? Writing about how these clumsy comments do not actually affect any specific or important aspects of your life can be a useful exercise. Seeing it written in black and white can convince your emotional brain that these words and actions are, indeed, insignificant.

The comments and questions people are most likely to take personally and respond to emotionally come from family and friends. You have already established that family and friends generally have good intentions, and their comments may well contain useful suggestions, even if they were delivered insensitively. It is possible to derive useful information from these comments, but only if you evaluate them objectively. By objectively evaluating these comments, you can determine which ideas are useful and which stem from their anxiety and thus can be safely ignored. You can then use the useful information in these comments to improve yourself or your plan.

When you evaluate the statements rationally as opposed to emotionally, you will be able to treat your family with respect and kindness, even when they make incorrect or impolite statements, since it is unlikely that they are doing so intentionally. Furthermore, there is no need for you to correct their erroneous statements. Though their mistakes may make them look foolish, they do not negatively impact you. In your notebook, determine which parts, if any, of the statements you have heard or expect to hear contain useful information. Analyzing a statement objectively and without emotion will enable you to identify the valuable aspects you can use to improve yourself, even if most of the statement is nonsense. If you express gratitude for the care and effort of a family member or friend, you will also be able to accept such statements calmly and improve your relationships with them, even if their comments and questions were not useful.

Preplanning your responses to seemingly judgmental comments and questions can prevent injury from mere words. A good strategy is to not engage with the question, either mentally or verbally. It does not mean ignoring the questioner, which will hurt feelings and increase tension, but rather shifting the conversation to a more constructive topic. You may have seen politicians and professors use this strategy by answering the question they want to answer, which is often only tangentially related to the question that was actually asked. In your notebook, write some responses to the comments and questions you have identified that can help move the conversation in a more productive, caring, and overall positive direction. Structure your responses to bring the conversation back to celebrating your accomplishments and their role in making them possible. As an example to a question regarding your postcollegiate plans, you might respond that your academic and personal growth in college has prepared you for a wide range of exciting opportunities, and you are grateful for their consistent support. Displaying confidence will also lessen their anxiety and their tendency to cross-examine. Having a prepared response or two is a very effective way to navigate family gatherings.

PURSUIT OF THE GOOD LIFE

Choosing the right path is always better than choosing the "right now" path. In fact, committing to a long-term trajectory before gathering the necessary information to determine whether it is the right path for you has almost no benefits. I cannot think of a single advantage. On the other hand, rushing can have disastrous consequences. The mistake of choosing an unsuitable career in order to get started more quickly will only lead you more rapidly toward an inferior destination and a lifetime of dissatisfaction. Taking the time needed to identify a promising trajectory, however, has numerous benefits. If you have a clear idea of what career will be most fulfilling for you, you will be able to continue on your path of self-improvement, to enjoy rewarding experiences, and to choose a future that will provide you with a lifetime of satisfaction and well-being. When you take the time to consider your best course of action, you will be fully prepared to handle the pressure you put on yourself and the pressure you feel from your family. However, you are in complete control of the impact of these pressures on your life, because their probing questions can only cause distress if you allow them. As a result, the comments of others, even if among those close to you, do not directly affect your life or well-being. There are no frustrating people, only people we allow to frustrate us. Understanding your family's compassionate intentions will allow you to disregard potentially unsettling comments and utilize the valuable information to improve your chances of success while simultaneously improving your relationships and well-being. This compassionate response will aid you in your pursuit of the good life.

KEY POINTS

- Completing a college degree is a significant milestone that deserves recognition and celebration.
- The transitionary period around college graduation causes uncertainty for students and their families, often resulting in counterproductive behaviors from family members that increase anxiety levels.
- Your family is likely genuinely concerned about your happiness and success but worried about any uncertainties in your plans.
- Critical questions from family can validate your nervous thoughts about your own next steps and further exacerbate anxiety.
- Some uncertainty about your future is normal and acceptable; you do not need a detailed map for your future when you finish college.

EPILOGUE

Next Steps

Congratulations! You have begun your pursuit of the good life—a state of flourishing in which your intellect is developed while enjoying positive well-being and life satisfaction. Through this book, I hope you have learned a great deal about yourself, your goals, and many approaches that can help you progress as you pursue the life satisfaction that is a hallmark of what Aristotle called "the Good Life." However, even the ancient masters who spent a lifetime pursuing the good life never achieved perfection and remained in pursuit until the very end. Similarly, it is unlikely that you have perfected your approach to life in such a way that you are never irritated or aggrieved by events or situations. In my opinion, the fact that we will be forever in pursuit of the good life is a blessing, not a curse. Continually reimagining ourselves leads to continual self-improvement, one of the great joys of life. Progress, not perfection, is the goal. The purpose of this final chapter is to guide your next steps on your journey toward the good life.

All the ideas in this book are variations on three foundational and interrelated themes: (1) constant and conscientious reevaluation of values and goals; (2) only progress and self-improvement matter, not achievements and outcomes; and (3) focusing only on desires and actions that are entirely within your control. Each of these themes is briefly described on the following pages and in detail in the books highlighted later in the chapter. I have attempted to organize the chapters by theme in the table of chapters on page 152, although you might notice that most chapters touch on more than one theme.

Values—Your core values are the guiding principles in your life. Your core values help you to distinguish right from wrong, to identify the appropriate actions to take in any given situation, and to identify appropriate goals and desires. Importantly, it is natural for our core values to be developed throughout our lives, as we will always be works in progress. Examining your core values regularly is crucial, since your values will change as your academic, cultural, and social knowledge expands. Additionally, it is vital to continually analyze your thoughts, desires, and actions to ensure they are aligned with your values.

Progress over outcomes—Life is a journey, not a destination, as the saying goes. Well-being and life satisfaction that is contingent on accomplishments is a recipe for disaster. Although society often associates achievement and awards with happiness, there is no rational basis supporting this assumption. Attaining your long-term goals takes months or years, while the moment of achievement occurs in an instant that few people take the time to enjoy. Consequently, well-being that depends on accomplishment suggests that happiness occurs only in a few moments that are preceded and followed by months of anxiety and dissatisfaction. Realigning your focus from accomplishments to personal progress, on the other hand, will allow you to experience continuous satisfaction and, paradoxically, will make it easier for you to achieve the accomplishments that society values. Every effort that improves your life is a success; self-improvement, not perfection, is the key to life satisfaction and well-being. Reframing extrinsic motivators into progress-oriented, intrinsically satisfying goals and avoiding peer comparisons are also included in this theme.

Control—The most effective way to pursue the good life is to focus your energy on activities that are under your complete control. The outcomes of the vast majority of activities are influenced by the actions of others or by chance. It is inevitable that some outcomes you wish would *not* occur nevertheless will occur, whereas other outcomes you wish would occur will not, regardless of your efforts. Allowing the outcome of events that are not under your complete control to impact your well-being or your progress on the path toward the good life is a fool's game. In contrast, if you control the outcome completely, you will always achieve your desired outcome. Hence, if you measure success by your level of effort toward a worthwhile goal aligned with your core values, which is in your complete control, you can never fail. Incidentally, this is both the definition of the Aristotelian Good Life and the most effective method of achieving success in modern society.

PLANNING YOUR OWN PATH TOWARD THE GOOD LIFE

Through your reading and practice, you likely have a better idea of what concepts and exercises currently work for you. The remainder of this chapter is devoted to helping you continue your pursuit of the good life beyond college. To begin, identify one or several lessons and approaches that you found particularly helpful. It might be helpful to document in your journal why these lessons were useful and how you can continue to apply them in the future. It may be beneficial to practice these approaches indefinitely. Continuous practice, however, can change your mindset so that you apply the approaches without needing to practice. In either case, continue practicing approaches as long as they remain beneficial in achieving life satisfaction, well-being, and other goals. A change in your current routine may be necessary if your current lessons are no longer effective or if a new obstacle arises that requires a different approach. This can be accomplished by adding new lessons or moving on from current lessons. Changes or additions should not be made too frequently since most approaches require practice before they become effective.

The emphasis throughout this book has been on practical approaches that can guide you in your pursuit of the good life while in college. There is an abundance of philosophy, psychology, and research behind all the lessons and approaches. You can, of course, continue to use the techniques you have learned to address specific hindrances in your life without a solid understanding of the theory behind them. Studying the underlying theories will, however, allow you to adapt and apply techniques more broadly and to novel situations. I have compiled a list of books that I have found particularly useful for understanding the foundations and theory, most of which also contain practical instructions.

VALUES	PROGRESS	CONTROL
Chapter 1: Why College?	Chapter 3: Overwhelming Opportunities	Chapter 1: Why College?
Chapter 2: Your Collegiate Self-Image	Chapter 6: Busyness Is Not Productive	Chapter 3: Overwhelming Opportunities
Chapter 4: Choose Friends Patiently	Chapter 7: Effective Studying	Chapter 4: Choose Friends Patiently
Chapter 5: Intrinsic Motivation	Chapter 8: Test Anxiety	Chapter 5: Intrinsic Motivation
Chapter 13: The Authentic Life	Chapter 10: Ask for Guidance	Chapter 7: Effective Studying
Chapter 16: After College?	Chapter 11: Grade Uncertainty	Chapter 9: Competitive Peers
	Chapter 13: The Authentic Life	Chapter 11: Grade Uncertainty
	Chapter 14: Uninteresting Courses	Chapter 12: Course Planning
	Chapter 15: Deep Projects	Chapter 14: Uninteresting Courses
		Chapter 16: After College?

FURTHER READINGS

The practices and exercises presented in this book are drawn from ancient philosophies like Stoicism and Epicureanism, modern psychology like cognitive behavioral therapy (which was founded on Stoic philosophy according to its founders, Aaron T. Beck and Albert Ellis), and human evolutionary biology. A list of the works that have influenced my thinking and practice in my pursuit of the good life follow. I have also included a brief description of each from my point of view. The book you are currently holding is a distillation of ideas and practices from these and other sources, adapted to address common problems facing students in higher education today. The texts listed here can help to guide your pursuit of the good life beyond the hallowed halls of your institution.

Ancient Texts

Enchiridion by Epictetus[1]

Enchiridion, also known as the *Handbook of Epictetus*, is a collection of practical guidelines for applying Stoic philosophy to daily life. There are fifty-three chapters, each only one or two paragraphs long, that describe how to achieve mental freedom and well-being in any circumstance. These practical entries are derived from the *Discourses of Epictetus*—some of which survive to this day and some have been lost to history—which are a written version of the lectures and teachings given by Epictetus and recorded by his student, Arrian of Nicomedia. The *Enchiridion* and the *Discourses* are an excellent introduction to Stoicism, written in a short, direct, almost brusque style that I find engaging and endearing. There are many translations available, and I am not endorsing one over another.

Meditations by Marcus Aurelius Antoninus[2]

Meditations is a brilliant and now classic work of philosophy that, to my understanding, was not written with the intention that others might read it. *Meditations* is the journal of Marcus Aurelius Antoninus, the emperor-philosopher of ancient Rome, written during a period of great upheaval. During the reign of Marcus Aurelius, there was a decades-long plague, wars with northern invaders, political treachery, and even treason. The journal documents how Marcus Aurelius lived according to his philosophical ideals while leading the largest empire of the time through this incredibly difficult era. For many people, *Meditations* is their first and only interaction with Stoicism. *Meditations* also provides a decent account of the history of the time as seen through the eyes of one person. I suggest reading *How to Think Like a Roman Emperor*, referenced later, prior to reading *Meditations* in order to put the writings of the emperor in context.

Letters and Philosophical Testaments by Seneca[3]

Seneca was a gifted statesman, playwright, and philosopher in the times just preceding Marcus Aurelius Antoninus. The life of Seneca, in addition to his philosophical writings, is also incredibly interesting. His writings and letters have been well preserved, likely due to his proximity to the Roman Emperor Nero (who forced Seneca to take his own life) and to his fame as a dramatist. Seneca writes in a flowing, rhythmic style that is a pleasure to read. He was also a very prolific writer. The most important contributions he made to philosophy focused on pursuing the good life and can be found both in philosophical treatises and in his letters to his friends.[4] The books that contain his writings are often organized around themes that commonly disrupt the well-being of people, including anger, grief, forgiveness, regret, and loss. It is difficult to find a topic Seneca did not address at least once in his massive collection of writings. The books and letters constitute both a theoretical and practical curriculum for studying Stoic philosophy.

Modern Books and Resources

CONTEMPORARY STOICISM

A Handbook for New Stoics: How to Thrive in a World out of Your Control by Massimo Pigliucci and Gregory Lopez[5]

This is a wonderfully simple and effective guide to the practical aspects of Stoicism. Furthermore, the core concepts of Stoicism and their connection to the techniques are explained in an accessible manner. The book is well-researched, meticulously organized, and a great action-based introduction to the philosophy and practice of Stoicism. I found the presentation in *A Handbook for New Stoics* so engaging that I used it as a model for this book. It is also my go-to book to address issues in my own life.

How to Think Like a Roman Emperor by Donald Robertson[6]

This is a fantastic book both because of its content and its entertaining style. This book focuses on the life and thinking of Marcus Aurelius Antoninus, the last of the "Five Good Emperors of Rome," a true philosopher king, and the author of *Meditations* described earlier. Robertson uses a combination of historical context and modern psychology (the author's professional expertise) to distill the ancient emperor's philosophy into useful exercises and mindsets that are relevant to life in modern times. I recommend reading this book prior to reading *Meditations* in order to put the ancient writings in context, to better understand the emperor's journey in Stoic philosophy, and to understand how he was able to utilize this philosophy effectively during remarkably trying times.

A Guide to the Good Life: The Ancient Art of Stoic Joy by William Irvine[7]

This is another well-written and engaging book that connects ancient Stoicism with modern living. This text is heavier on the core tenets of the philosophy—as opposed to guidance in practical application—than some of the other books suggested. Nevertheless, there is an emphasis on connecting theory and practice and several specific guides can be found throughout. The theory, written for a nonacademic audience, is easily understandable so that anyone can connect the philosophical doctrines to living a meaningful and happy life.

The Obstacle Is the Way, *Ego Is the Enemy*, and the *Daily Stoic* website (https://dailystoic.com), by Ryan Holiday[8]

The books by Ryan Holiday, some of which are coauthored by Stephen Hanselman, deliver accessible and passionate philosophical and practical teachings. As the title of the first book suggests, the major focus of these books is changing your mindset so that you can not only overcome obstacles, but also turn them into opportunities. As I understand them, the two books are aimed at improving leadership, traditional success, and making a difference in the world. As an aside, the writing style of these books is not particularly engaging for me. This is not an argument against reading them; you should. They have excellent and well-researched content and the writing style is loved by many thousands of people. Through this aside, I can discuss the importance of books like this, including the one you are holding. Most of these modern books function more like teachers than like research articles. Rather than discovering novel ideas, the authors interpret existing knowledge and determine what to present and how to present it. The style of presentation that you find most engaging is likely different from mine and I encourage you to read these books for their content and possibly for their style. Considering their popularity, you are likely to appreciate their presentation style as well.

CONTEMPORARY PSYCHOLOGY

***Authentic Happiness: Using the New Positive Psychology to Realize Your Potential for Lasting Fulfillment* by Martin E. P. Seligman**[9]
The study and practice of psychology is primarily concerned with the causes and treatments of mental states that make life miserable. The field of positive psychology, cofounded by Dr. Seligman and described beautifully for a nonacademic audience in this book, focuses on the opposite state of human mentality. The field of positive psychology aims to understand and cultivate positive emotions, to build virtue and resilience, and to find lasting fulfillment through meaning and purpose. The book by Dr. Seligman describes both the underlying scientific evidence as well as practical exercises to build authentic happiness by identifying and developing your fundamental strengths and using them in your daily life. This is a fascinating read and provides useful strategies for harnessing positive emotion and dissipating negative emotion. In full disclosure, Professor Seligman is on the faculty of the University of Pennsylvania, where I also teach. However, I do not believe this has affected my appreciation of his work.

***Grit: The Power of Passion and Perseverance* by Angela Duckworth**[10]
Although the main point of this book and the research behind it seem like they should be obvious—that hard work and perseverance are better predictors of success than talent—I am not sure that they are. Before reading this book, I had never considered many of the ideas that now seem obvious. I certainly did not apply these ideas to the improvement of my own life. There are many examples of "gritty" success stories that many readers find both informative and motivating, although there are more examples than necessary in my opinion. Nevertheless, the gem of this work lies in the compilation of decades of psychological research and the practical strategies for increasing motivation, passion, and perseverance at school or at work. Professor Duckworth is also a colleague at the University of Pennsylvania whose work I recommend.

APPENDIX

Philosophical Background

The practical approaches and theoretical knowledge presented in this book can be used to address immediate difficulties as well as to influence habits, dispositions, and your character in general. That is, each concept and approach could be used to reduce anxiety in the present moment, to develop a strategy to moderate the impact of future obstacles, or to modify your perspective and mental approach to challenging situations in general. Through learning the theory and practicing the approaches, you can move from handling difficult situations as they arise, to reducing the negative impact of difficult situations in general, to changing your outlook so that you see "difficult" situations as opportunities. The journey through these stages is a lifelong process, but perfection is not the goal. Any effort that improves your life today and into the future is a success. Improving, not perfecting, your mindset and actions is the key to maximizing your well-being, life satisfaction, and potential for success in college and beyond.

All the ideas and practices rest on one foundational concept: focusing your efforts on self-improvement gives you the best chance for life satisfaction, well-being, and academic success. Conversely, allowing the outcomes of your efforts to determine your well-being will undoubtedly lead to frustration and misery. The vast majority of "outcomes"—from the grade you receive in a course to winning awards to making and maintaining friendships—are influenced by other people's actions. In other words, you do not have complete control over the *results* of your efforts. Consequently, there will always be some outcomes you wish would not happen, but they do, and other outcomes you wish would happen, but they do not. It is also important to note that even when you achieve what you hope for, the feeling of satisfaction is transient and soon gives way to a longing for the next triumph, which may or may not happen (see figure in chapter 11). Nevertheless, it is common for students to allow grades, awards, and recognition to determine their well-being and life satisfaction.

Defining success as a quality effort toward a worthwhile goal will always lead to a sense of well-being, since you have control over both the goal and the level of effort. This book aims to help you change your perspective so that your efforts—not the outcomes—determine your well-being and life satisfaction. As an interesting and important aside, focusing solely on your effort to learn the course material will simultaneously increase your chances of earning high grades (and winning awards and receiving recognition).

"THE GOOD LIFE" FROM MY PERSPECTIVE

A few of the concepts in this book, including the central concept of "the Good Life," are somewhat ambiguous. Different people define many of these concepts differently, and their definitions may even continue to evolve throughout a person's lifetime. Some readers have suggested, however, that a more concrete description of these concepts would be helpful for their progress, especially as they embark on their own pursuit of the good life. In the following sections, I have outlined my current perspective of what it means to pursue the good life and associated concepts such as ethical actions, virtue, and intrinsic motivation. It is important to reiterate that these definitions represent my current ideas about these concepts (I am actively pursuing the good life; I have not attained it), that you will develop your definitions as you progress on *your* pursuit of the good life, and that there are formal academic definitions of most of these concepts that may or may not align with mine. I include my perspective here to provide context from which you may better understand the lessons and as a starting point from which you can develop your definitions.

The Good Life

From my perspective, the good life is meaningful, satisfying, and lived with a continual sense of personal well-being. The good life is pursued by living virtuously. All people define "living virtuously" differently, but for most, it entails thinking, acting, and behaving following humanity's better nature. In other words, following the advice of the metaphorical angel on your shoulder and acting counter to the advice of the metaphorical devil. According to my experience, ethical thoughts and actions are based on the capacity for reason, the instinctual desire for self-improvement, respect for courageous acts, a predisposition toward justice, and quality interpersonal relationships. These five concepts serve as guideposts in my pursuit of the good life and constitute the pillars of my core values.

Ethical Thoughts, Actions, and Behaviors

For most people, the foundations of ethical thinking, actions, and behaviors are innate, intrinsically motivated, and under their complete control. For example, neither societal rewards nor external recognition are necessary to achieve the sense of well-being and satisfaction associated with spending quality time with friends and family, improving your performance through hard work, or attempting to rectify an injustice. The foundations of virtuous thoughts and actions are intrinsically motivated—these actions make you happy simply by doing them, not because of what you gain as a reward for doing them. The pursuit of the good life, in my opinion, is attaining life satisfaction and well-being by cultivating these ethical behaviors. In other words, living virtuously means aspiring to become an excellent human being, which comes with the reward of a life of satisfaction and well-being.

Focus on What Is in Your *Complete Control*

This does not mean that you should not dream big; you should make decisions that will enable you to achieve great things. However, adjusting your motivations to focus exclusively on what you can control completely will improve the quality of your decisions as well as the probability of reaching your goals. A key to pursuing the good life is to value only what is valuable. Because assigning value to thoughts and actions is entirely within your control, it is ultimately within your power to pursue the good life. Actions and behaviors of high value are intrinsically motivated, within your complete control, and align with your core values (i.e., what you define as ethical thoughts and actions). By accurately assessing the value of your thoughts and actions, you can avoid suffering, grief, and anxiety and achieve life satisfaction and well-being.

Virtuous Thoughts and Actions Are Intrinsically Motivated

The motivation for most actions can come from both intrinsic and extrinsic sources. For example, you might drive your sister to football practice both because you fear punishment (extrinsic motivation) and because you genuinely care about the well-being of your family (intrinsic motivation). People who carry out actions inspired by intrinsic factors have a better quality of life and are more satisfied with their lives, regardless of the views of others. By contrast, extrinsically motivated thoughts and actions, such as seeking external validation or avoiding the disapproval of others, often result in suffering, grief, and anxiety. Examples of extrinsic motivators include the desire for academic, career, material, and interpersonal success (not to worry—these are achieved *much* more effectively through intrinsic motivation; see chapter 5). Motivation that comes from external sources can negatively affect feelings of well-being and life satisfaction since the ultimate outcome is not within your complete control. Pursuing the good life involves limiting the influence of extrinsic motivations on your well-being, even when it is impossible to ignore them completely. Initially, this may seem not very comforting, but being motivated exclusively by intrinsic factors is genuinely liberating and, ironically, will result in greater academic, material, and interpersonal success than extrinsic motivation, according to modern research.

Intrinsic motivators are those driven by internal objectives that are inherently satisfying. Intrinsically motivated actions are those that you want to do regardless of the possibility of gaining recognition, money, grades, or other benefits. For example, it is exciting and enjoyable to listen to a beautiful piece of music (intrinsic motivation), not because you will earn an award for your listening skills (extrinsic motivation). Intrinsic motivations are generally under your complete control and are progress oriented, as opposed to outcome oriented. Enjoying music is within your control—there are many great pieces of music you can listen to—and it does not have an end goal—there is always more enjoyment to be had through good music. Incidentally, most research suggests that intrinsically motivated actions are more likely to lead to external successes in areas like academics, careers, material gains, and social relationships than externally motivated actions.[1]

NOTES

INTRODUCTION

1. Aristotle, *Nicomachean Ethics*, trans. Terence Irwin, 2nd ed. (Indianapolis, IN: Hackett, 1999). See Part VI: Philosophical Background.

2. Diogenes Laertius, *Lives of the Eminent Philosophers*, ed. Jim Miller, trans. Pamela Mensch (New York: Oxford University Press, 2018).

CHAPTER ONE

1. Dante Alighieri, *The Divine Comedy of Dante Alighieri*, trans. Courtney Langdon (Cambridge, MA: Harvard University Press, 1920).

2. Michael A. Campion and Robert G. Lord, "A Control Systems Conceptualization of the Goal-Setting and Changing Process," *Organizational Behavior and Human Performance* 30, no. 2 (1982): 265–87; Cheryl J. Travers, Dominique Morisano, and Edwin A. Locke, "Self-Reflection, Growth Goals, and Academic Outcomes: A Qualitative Study," *British Journal of Educational Psychology* 85, no. 2 (2015): 224–41; Ainslea Cross and David Sheffield, "Mental Contrasting as a Behaviour Change Technique: A Systematic Review Protocol Paper of Effects, Mediators and Moderators on Health," *Systematic Reviews* 5, no. 1 (2016): 1–6.

3. W.-C. Mau, R. Hitchcock, and C. Calvert, "High School Students' Career Plans: The Influence of Others' Expectations," *Professional School Counseling* 2, no. 2 (1998): 161–66; Kay Herting Wahl and Anne Blackhurst, 'Factors Affecting the Occupational and Educational Aspirations of Children and Adolescents," *Professional School Counseling* 3, no. 5 (2000): 367.

4. Joseph Campbell, *The Hero's Journey: Joseph Campbell on His Life and Work*, ed. Phil Cousineau (San Francisco: Harper San Francisco, 1991).

5. W.-C. Mau, R. Hitchcock, and C. Calvert, "High School Students' Career Plans: The Influence of Others' Expectations," *Professional School Counseling* 2, no. 2 (1998): 161–66; Kay Herting Wahl and Anne Blackhurst, "Factors Affecting the Occupational and Educational Aspirations of Children and Adolescents," *Professional School Counseling* 3, no. 5 (2000): 367; Paul Dolan,

Tessa Peasgood, and Mathew White, "Do We Really Know What Makes Us Happy? A Review of the Economic Literature on the Factors Associated with Subjective Well-Being," *Journal of Economic Psychology* 29, no. 1 (2008): 94–122; Nattavudh Powdthavee, Warn N. Lekfuangfu, and Mark Wooden, "What's the Good of Education on Our Overall Quality of Life? A Simultaneous Equation Model of Education and Life Satisfaction for Australia," *Journal of Behavioral and Experimental Economics* 54 (2015): 10–21; Robert A. Witter, Morris Okun, William Stock, and Marilyn Haring, "Education and Subjective Well-Being: A Meta-Analysis," *Educational Evaluation and Policy Analysis* 6, no. 2 (1984): 165–73.

    6. Aristotle, *Nicomachean Ethics*, ed. Terence Irwin, 2nd ed. (Indianapolis, IN: Hackett, 1999).

    7. David Strickland and Carol Strickland, "My Sociology: The Challenge of Transforming Classroom Culture from a Focus on Grades to a Focus on Learning," *The Journal of Public and Professional Sociology* 5, no. 2 (2013): 4; Yi Guang Lin, Wilbert J. McKeachie, and Yung Che Kim, "College Student Intrinsic and/or Extrinsic Motivation and Learning," *Learning and Individual Differences* 13, no. 3 (2003): 251–58; Andrew N. Christopher, Liliane Saliba, and Erik J. Deadmarsh, "Materialism and Well-Being: The Mediating Effect of Locus of Control," *Personality and Individual Differences* 46, no. 7 (2009): 682–86; Todd B. Kashdan and William E. Breen, "Materialism and Diminished Well-Being: Experiential Avoidance as a Mediating Mechanism," *Journal of Social and Clinical Psychology* 26, no. 5 (2007): 521–39; John Mark Froiland, Emily Oros, Liana Smith, and Tyrell Hirchert, "Intrinsic Motivation to Learn: The Nexus between Psychological Health and Academic Success," *Contemporary School Psychology* 16, no. 1 (2014): 91–100.

CHAPTER TWO

    1. Marcus Aurelius, *Meditations*, trans. J. Boulton and David Widger (Project Gutenberg, 2021), www.gutenberg.org/cache/epub/2680/pg2680.

    2. R. G. Simmons, F. Rosenberg, and M. Rosenberg, "Disturbance in the Self-Image at Adolescence," *American Sociological Review* 38, no. 5 (1973): 553–68; Susan Harter, "The Development of Self-Representations," in *Handbook of Child Psychology: Social, Emotional, and Personality Development*, ed. W. Damon and N. Eisenberg (Hoboken, NJ: John Wiley & Sons, 1998), 553–617.

    3. Toni Morrison, *Beloved: A Novel* (New York: Vintage, 2004).

    4. Susan Harter, "The Development of Self-Representations," in *Handbook of Child Psychology: Social, Emotional, and Personality Development*,

ed. W. Damon and N. Eisenberg (Hoboken, NJ: John Wiley & Sons, 1998), 553–617.

5. Peter J. Burke, "The Self: Measurement Requirements from an Interactionist Perspective," *Social Psychology Quarterly* 43, no. 1 (1980): 18.

6. Jay T. Knippen and Thad B. Green, "Asking for Positive Reinforcement," *Journal of Workplace Learning* 9, no. 5 (1997): 163–68.

7. Roy F. Baumeister and Kathleen D. Vohs, "Narcissism as Addiction to Esteem," *Psychological Inquiry* 12, no. 4 (2001): 206–10; Brad J. Bushman, Scott J. Moeller, and Jennifer Crocker, "Sweets, Sex, or Self-Esteem? Comparing the Value of Self-Esteem Boosts with Other Pleasant Rewards," *Journal of Personality* 79, no. 5 (2011): 993–1012.

8. Joar Vittersø and Yngvil Søholt, "Life Satisfaction Goes with Pleasure and Personal Growth Goes with Interest: Further Arguments for Separating Hedonic and Eudaimonic Well-Being," *The Journal of Positive Psychology* 6, no. 4 (2011): 326–35.

9. Louise C. Hawkley and John P. Capitanio, "Perceived Social Isolation, Evolutionary Fitness and Health Outcomes: A Lifespan Approach," *Philosophical Transactions of the Royal Society of London, Series B, Biological Sciences* 370, no. 1669 (2015): 20140114; Maxine Weinstein and Meredith A. Lane, *Sociality, Hierarchy, Health: Comparative Biodemography: A Collection of Papers* (Washington, DC: National Academies Press, 2014).

CHAPTER THREE

1. Lucius Annaeus Seneca, *Moral Letters to Lucilius—Letters from a Stoic*, trans. Richard M. Gummere (Cambridge, MA: Loeb Classical Library Edition, 1915).

2. Etty Hillesum, K. A. D. Smelik, and Arnold Pomerans, *Etty: The Letters and Diaries of Etty Hillesum, 1941–1943* (Grand Rapids, MI: William B. Eerdmans Publishing, 2002).

3. Christopher J. Budnick, Arielle P. Rogers, and Larissa K. Barber, "The Fear of Missing out at Work: Examining Costs and Benefits to Employee Health and Motivation," *Computers in Human Behavior* 104 (2020): 106161; Andrew K. Przybylski, Kou Murayama, Cody R. DeHaan, and Valerie Gladwell, "Motivational, Emotional, and Behavioral Correlates of Fear of Missing Out," *Computers in Human Behavior* 29, no. 4 (2013): 1841–48; Marina Milyavskaya, Mark Saffran, Nora Hope, and Richard Koestner, "Fear of Missing Out: Prevalence, Dynamics, and Consequences of Experiencing FOMO," *Motivation and Emotion* 42, no. 5 (2018): 725–37.

4. Beckett A. Broh, "Linking Extracurricular Programming to Academic Achievement: Who Benefits and Why?" *Sociology of Education* 75, no. 1 (2002): 69–95; Christopher B. Swanson, "Spending Time or Investing Time? Involvement in High School Curricular and Extracurricular Activities as Strategic Action," *Rationality and Society* 14, no. 4 (2002): 431–71; William G. Camp, "Participation in Student Activities and Achievement: A Covariance Structural Analysis," *The Journal of Educational Research* 83, no. 5 (1990): 271–78.

5. K. Rowa, "Atychiphobia (Fear of Failure)," in *Phobias: The Psychology of Irrational Fear*, ed. Irena Milosevic and Randi E. McCabe (Westport, CT: Greenwood, 2015).

6. Anne M. Finucane, "The Effect of Fear and Anger on Selective Attention," *Emotion* 11, no. 4 (2011): 970–74.

CHAPTER FOUR

1. *Æesop's Fables*, trans. V. S. Vernon Jones (London: William Heinemann, 1912).

2. Liesl M. Heinrich and Eleonora Gullone, "The Clinical Significance of Loneliness: A Literature Review," *Clinical Psychology Review* 26, no. 6 (2006): 695–718.

3. Javier Yanguas, Sacramento Pinazo-Henandis, and Francisco José Tarazona-Santabalbina, "The Complexity of Loneliness," *Acta Bio Medica: Atenei Parmensis* 89, no. 2 (2018): 302.

4. Carolyn E. Cutrona, "Transition to College: Loneliness and the Process of Social Adjustment," in *Loneliness: A Sourcebook of Current Theory, Research and Practice*, ed. L. A. Peplau and D. Pearlman (New York: Wiley Interscience, 1982), 291–309; Ladd Wheeler, Harry Reis, and John B. Nezlek, "Loneliness, Social Interaction, and Sex Roles," *Journal of Personality and Social Psychology* 45, no. 4 (1983): 943–53.

5. L. A. Peplau and D. Perlman, *Loneliness: A Sourcebook of Current Theory, Research and Therapy* (New York: Wiley Interscience, 1982).

6. George Washington, *The Writings of George Washington, Vol. I (1748–1757)*, ed. Worthington Chauncey Ford (New York and London: G. P. Putnam's Sons, 1889–1893).

7. Louise C. Hawkley and John P. Capitanio, "Perceived Social Isolation, Evolutionary Fitness and Health Outcomes: A Lifespan Approach," *Philosophical Transactions of the Royal Society of London, Series B, Biological Sciences* 370, no. 1669 (2015): 20140114; Maxine Weinstein and Meredith A.

Lane, *Sociality, Hierarchy, Health: Comparative Biodemography: A Collection of Papers* (Washington, DC: National Academies Press, 2014).

8. Louise C. Hawkley and John T. Cacioppo, "Loneliness Matters: A Theoretical and Empirical Review of Consequences and Mechanisms," *Annals of Behavioral Medicine: A Publication of the Society of Behavioral Medicine* 40, no. 2 (2010): 218–27.

9. L. A. Peplau and D. Perlman, *Loneliness: A Sourcebook of Current Theory, Research and Therapy* (New York: Wiley Interscience, 1982); Carolyn E. Cutrona, "Transition to College: Loneliness and the Process of Social Adjustment," in *Loneliness: A Sourcebook of Current Theory, Research and Practice*, ed. L. A. Peplau and D. Pearlman (New York: Wiley Interscience, 1982), 291–309; James J. Ponzetti, "Loneliness among College Students," *Family Relations* 39, no. 3 (1990): 336–40.

10. Marco Iacoboni, "Imitation, Empathy, and Mirror Neurons," *Annual Review of Psychology* 60, no. 1 (2008): 653–70.

11. Epictetus, *Discourses, Fragments, Handbook*, trans. Robin Hard (New York: Oxford World Classics, 2014).

12. Chris Williams and Anne Garland, "Identifying and Challenging Unhelpful Thinking," *Advances in Psychiatric Treatment* 8, no. 5 (2002): 377–86.

13. Marco Iacoboni, "Imitation, Empathy, and Mirror Neurons," *Annual Review of Psychology* 60, no. 1 (2008): 653–70.

CHAPTER FIVE

1. Marcus Aurelius, *Meditations*, trans. J. Boulton and David Widger (Project Gutenberg, 2021), www.gutenberg.org/cache/epub/2680/pg2680.

2. Todd B. Kashdan and William E. Breen, "Materialism and Diminished Well-Being: Experiential Avoidance as a Mediating Mechanism," *Journal of Social and Clinical Psychology* 26, no. 5 (2007): 521–39; Andrew N. Christopher, Terell P. Lasane, Jordan D. Troisi, and Lora E. Park, "Materialism, Defensive and Assertive Self-Presentational Tactics, and Life Satisfaction," *Journal of Social and Clinical Psychology* 26, no. 10 (2007): 1145–62; Aaron Ahuvia, "If Money Doesn't Make Us Happy, Why Do We Act as If It Does?" *Journal of Economic Psychology* 29, no. 4 (2008): 491–507.

3. Andrew N. Christopher, Liliane Saliba, and Eric J. Deadmarsh, "Materialism and Well-Being: The Mediating Effect of Locus of Control," *Personality and Individual Differences* 46, no. 7 (2009): 682–86; Todd B. Kashdan and William E. Breen, "Materialism and Diminished Well-Being: Experiential

Avoidance as a Mediating Mechanism," *Journal of Social and Clinical Psychology* 26, no. 5 (2007): 521–39.

4. Christian Commission for Camp and Defense Communities, *A Book of Prayers for the Armed Forces by Commission on Worship of the Federal Council of the Churches of Christ in America* (Winfield, KS: White/Walnut Valley Books, 1944).

5. Edward L. Deci, *Intrinsic Motivation* (New York: Plenum Press, 1975).

6. Maureen J. Findley and Harris M. Cooper, "Locus of Control and Academic Achievement: A Literature Review," *Journal of Personality and Social Psychology* 44, no. 2 (1983): 419–27.

7. Maria Miceli and Cristiano Castelfranchi, "Nature and Mechanisms of Loss of Motivation," *Review of General Psychology* 4, no. 3 (2000): 238–63.

8. Joseph R. Ferrari, "Self-Handicapping by Procrastinators: Protecting Self-Esteem, Social-Esteem, or Both?" *Journal of Research in Personality* 25, no. 3 (1991): 245–61.

9. C. G. Crocker, "Frankford," *Delmarva News*, December 7, 1967.

10. Edward L. Deci, *Intrinsic Motivation* (New York: Plenum Press, 1975).

11. Birgit Spinath and Ricarda Steinmayr, "The Roles of Competence Beliefs and Goal Orientations for Change in Intrinsic Motivation," *Journal of Educational Psychology* 104, no. 4 (2012): 1135–48.

12. John Mark Froiland, Emily Oros, Liana Smith, and Tyrell Hirchert, "Intrinsic Motivation to Learn: The Nexus between Psychological Health and Academic Success," *Contemporary School Psychology* 16, no. 1 (2014): 91–100.

13. David Strickland and Carol Strickland, "My Sociology: The Challenge of Transforming Classroom Culture from a Focus on Grades to a Focus on Learning," *The Journal of Public and Professional Sociology* 5, no. 2 (2013): 4; Yi-Guang Lin, Wilbert J. McKeachie, and Yung Che Kim, "College Student Intrinsic and/or Extrinsic Motivation and Learning," *Learning and Individual Differences* 13, no 3 (2003): 251–58.

14. Rabia Khalaila, "The Relationship between Academic Self-Concept, Intrinsic Motivation, Test Anxiety, and Academic Achievement among Nursing Students: Mediating and Moderating Effects," *Nurse Education Today* 35, no. 3 (2015): 432–38.

15. Brian S. Rosner, *The Consolations of Theology* (Grand Rapids, MI: William B. Eerdmans, 2008).

16. Epictetus, *Discourses, Fragments, Handbook*, trans. Robin Hard (New York: Oxford World Classics, 2014).

17. Maureen J. Findley and Harris M. Cooper, "Locus of Control and Academic Achievement: A Literature Review," *Journal of Personality and Social*

Psychology 44, no. 2 (1983): 419–27; Timothy Z. Keith, Sheila M. Pottebaum, and Steve Eberhart, "Effects of Self-Concept and Locus of Control on Academic Achievement: A Large-Sample Path Analysis," *Journal of Psychoeducational Assessment* 4, no. 1 (1986): 61–72; Michael A. Kirkpatrick, Kathryn Stant, Shonta Downes, and Leatah Gaither, "Perceived Locus of Control and Academic Performance: Broadening the Construct's Applicability," *Journal of College Student Development* 49, no. 5 (2008): 486–96; Randy Carden, Courtney Bryant, and Rebekah Moss, "Locus of Control, Test Anxiety, Academic Procrastination, and Achievement among College Students," *Psychological Reports* 95, no. 2 (2004): 581–82.

18. David Strickland and Carol Strickland, "My Sociology: The Challenge of Transforming Classroom Culture from a Focus on Grades to a Focus on Learning," *The Journal of Public and Professional Sociology* 5, no. 2 (2013): 4; Yi-Guang Lin, Wilbert J. McKeachie, and Yung Che Kim, "College Student Intrinsic and/or Extrinsic Motivation and Learning," *Learning and Individual Differences* 13, no 3 (2003): 251–58.

CHAPTER SIX

1. Marcus Aurelius, *Meditations*, trans. J. Boulton and David Widger (Project Gutenberg, 2021), www.gutenberg.org/cache/epub/2680/pg2680.

2. Silvia Bellezza, Neeru Paharia, and Anat Keinan, "Conspicuous Consumption of Time: When Busyness and Lack of Leisure Time Become a Status Symbol," *Journal of Consumer Research* 44, no. 1 (2017): 118–38; Anat Keinan, Silvia Bellezza, and Neeru Paharia, "The Symbolic Value of Time," *Current Opinion in Psychology* 26 (2019): 58–61.

3. Susan Drew and Ruth Paradice, "Time, Women and Well-Being," *Feminism and Psychology* 6, no. 4 (1996): 563–68.

4. Timothy D. Wilson, David A. Reinhard, Erin C. Westgate, Daniel T. Gilbert, Nicole Ellerbeck, Cheryl Hahn, Casey L. Brown, and Adi Shaked, "Just Think: The Challenges of the Disengaged Mind," *Science* 345, no. 6192 (2014): 75–77.

5. Rick E. Ingram and Philip C. Kendall, "The Cognitive Side of Anxiety," *Cognitive Therapy and Research* 11, no. 5 (1987): 523–36.

6. Michael W. Vasey and Thomas D. Borkovec, "A Catastrophizing Assessment of Worrisome Thoughts," *Cognitive Therapy and Research* 16, no. 5 (1992): 505–20.

7. Timothy D. Wilson, David A. Reinhard, Erin C. Westgate, Daniel T. Gilbert, Nicole Ellerbeck, Cheryl Hahn, Casey L. Brown, and Adi Shaked,

"Just Think: The Challenges of the Disengaged Mind," *Science* 345, no. 6192 (2014): 75–77.

8. Karlene Kerfoot, "Beyond Busyness: Creating Slack in the Organization," *Nursing Economics* 24, no. 3 (2006): 168–70.

CHAPTER SEVEN

1. Lucius Annaeus Seneca, *Moral Letters to Lucilius—Letters from a Stoic*, trans. Richard M. Gummere (Cambridge, MA: Loeb Classical Library, 1915).

2. Beckett A. Broh, "Linking Extracurricular Programming to Academic Achievement: Who Benefits and Why?" *Sociology of Education* 75, no. 1 (2002): 69–95; Christopher B. Swanson, "Spending Time or Investing Time? Involvement in High School Curricular and Extracurricular Activities as Strategic Action," *Rationality and Society* 14, no. 4 (2002): 431–71; William G. Camp, "Participation in Student Activities and Achievement: A Covariance Structural Analysis," *The Journal of Educational Research* 83, no. 5 (1990): 271–78.

3. Michael J. Telch, David P. Valentiner, Doron Ilai, Paula R. Young, Mark B. Powers, and Jasper A. J. Smits, "Fear Activation and Distraction during the Emotional Processing of Claustrophobic Fear," *Journal of Behavior Therapy and Experimental Psychiatry* 35, no. 3 (2004): 219–32; Sadia Najmi, Bradley C. Riemann, and Daniel M. Wegner, "Managing Unwanted Intrusive Thoughts in Obsessive-Compulsive Disorder: Relative Effectiveness of Suppression, Focused Distraction, and Acceptance," *Behaviour Research and Therapy* 47, no. 6 (2009): 494–503.

4. Marcus Aurelius, *Meditations*, trans. Robin Hard (New York: Oxford University Press, 2011).

5. Bruce C. Wittmaier, "Test Anxiety and Study Habits," *The Journal of Educational Research* 65, no. 8 (1972): 352–54.

6. Eric Depreeuw and Hubert de Neve, "Test Anxiety Can Harm Your Health: Some Conclusions Based on a Student Typology," in *Anxiety: Recent Developments in Cognitive, Psychophysiological, and Health Research*, ed. Donald G. Forgays, Tytus Sosnowski, and Kazimierz Wrzesniewski (New York: Taylor & Francis, 1992), 211–28.

7. Graeme Stewart, Tricia Anne Seifert, and Carol Rolheiser, "Anxiety and Self-Efficacy's Relationship with Undergraduate Students' Perceptions of the Use of Metacognitive Writing Strategies," *The Canadian Journal for the Scholarship of Teaching and Learning* 6, no. 1 (2015).

8. Amelia Earhart, The Official Licensing Website of Amelia Earhart, www.ameliaearhart.com/Quotes (accessed February 24, 2020).

9. Bruce C. Wittmaier, "Test Anxiety and Study Habits," *The Journal of Educational Research* 65, no. 8 (1972): 352–54; Sigmund Tobias, "Anxiety and Cognitive Processing of Instruction," in *Self-Related Cognitions in Anxiety and Motivation*, ed. Ralf Schwarzer (New York: Psychology Press, 1986).

CHAPTER EIGHT

1. Lucius Annaeus Seneca, *Moral Letters to Lucilius—Letters from a Stoic*, trans. Richard M. Gummere (Cambridge, MA: Loeb Classical Library, 1915).

2. Michael W. Vasey and Thomas D. Borkovec, "A Catastrophizing Assessment of Worrisome Thoughts," *Cognitive Therapy and Research* 16, no. 5 (1992): 505–20; Tom Foulsham, Rana Alan, and Alan Kingstone, "Scrambled Eyes? Disrupting Scene Structure Impedes Focal Processing and Increases Bottom-up Guidance," *Attention, Perception, and Psychophysics* 73, no. 7 (2011): 2008–25.

3. Beyon Miloyan, Nancy A. Pachana, and Thomas Suddendorf, "The Future Is Here: A Review of Foresight Systems in Anxiety and Depression," *Cognition and Emotion* 28, no. 5 (2014): 795–810.

4. Weare A. Zwemer and Jerry L. Deffenbacher, "Irrational Beliefs, Anger, and Anxiety," *Journal of Counseling Psychology* 31, no. 3 (1984): 391–93.

5. Manuel G. Calvo and Michael W. Eysenck, "Anxiety and Performance: The Processing Efficiency Theory," *Cognition and Emotion* 6, no. 6 (1992): 409–34; Jeri Wine, "Test Anxiety and Direction of Attention," *Psychological Bulletin* 76, no. 2 (1971): 92–104.

6. Oliver Wilhelm, Andrea Hildebrandt, and Klaus Oberauer, "What Is Working Memory Capacity, and How Can We Measure It?" *Frontiers in Psychology* 4 (2013): e00433.

7. George A. Miller, "The Magical Number Seven, Plus or Minus Two: Some Limits on Our Capacity for Processing Information," *Psychological Review* 63, no. 2 (1956): 81–97.

8. Jeri Wine, "Test Anxiety and Direction of Attention," *Psychological Bulletin* 76, no. 2 (1971): 92–104; Manuel G. Calvo and Michael W. Eysenck, "Anxiety and Performance: The Processing Efficiency Theory," *Cognition and Emotion* 6, no. 6 (1992): 409–34.

9. David Strickland and Carol Strickland, "My Sociology: The Challenge of Transforming Classroom Culture from a Focus on Grades to a Focus on Learning," *The Journal of Public and Professional Sociology* 5, no. 2 (2013): 4; Yi-Guang Lin, Wilbert J. McKeachie, and Yung Che Kim, "College Student Intrinsic and/or Extrinsic Motivation and Learning," *Learning and Individual*

Differences 13, no. 3 (2003): 251–58; John Mark Froiland, Emily Oros, Liana Smith, and Tyrell Hirchert, "Intrinsic Motivation to Learn: The Nexus between Psychological Health and Academic Success," *Contemporary School Psychology* 16, no. 1 (2014): 91–100.

10. Tom Foulsham, Rana Alan, and Alan Kingstone, "Scrambled Eyes? Disrupting Scene Structure Impedes Focal Processing and Increases Bottom-up Guidance," *Attention, Perception, and Psychophysics* 73, no. 7 (2011): 2008–25.

CHAPTER NINE

1. Epictetus, *The Discourses as Reported by Arrian, the Manual, and Fragments*, trans. W. A. Oldfather (London: William Heinemann, 1925).

2. Adnan Adil, Sadaf Ameer, and Saba Ghayas, "Impact of Academic Psychological Capital on Academic Achievement among University Undergraduates: Roles of Flow and Self-Handicapping Behavior," *PsyCh Journal* 9, no. 1 (2020): 56–66.

3. Timothy Ferriss, *The 4-Hour Workweek: Escape 9-5, Live Anywhere, and Join the New Rich* (New York: Crown Publishers, 2007).

4. Louise C. Hawkley and John P. Capitanio, "Perceived Social Isolation, Evolutionary Fitness and Health Outcomes: A Lifespan Approach," *Philosophical Transactions of the Royal Society of London—Biological Sciences* 370, no. 1669 (2015): 20140114; Maxine Weinstein and Meredith A. Lane, *Sociality, Hierarchy, Health: Comparative Biodemography: A Collection of Papers* (Washington, DC: National Academies Press, 2014).

5. Robert Hamm, "Negative Will, Self-Image, and Personality Dysfunction," *Psychoanalytic Review* 96, no. 1 (2009): 55–82; E. Goffman, *The Presentation of Self in Everyday Life* (Garden City, NY: Doubleday, 1959).

6. Paul Black and Dylan Wiliam, "Assessment and Classroom Learning," *Assessment in Education: Principles, Policy and Practice* 21, no. 1 (1998): 7–74; J. R. L. Swain, "The Nature and Assessment of Scientific Explorations in the Classroom," *School Science Review* 72, no. 260 (1991): 65–77; Dianne M. Tice, "The Social Motivations of People with Low Self-Esteem," in *Self-Esteem: The Plenum Series in Social/Clinical Psychology*, ed. R. F. Baumeister (Boston: Springer, 1993), 37–53.

7. Anita H. G. M. Belapurkar, "Understanding Self and Its Importance in Education," *Scholarly Research Journal for Interdisciplinary Studies* 4, no. 25 (2016): 2433–39.

8. Marcus Aurelius, *Meditations*, trans. Robin Hard (New York: Oxford University Press, 2011).

9. Pieternel Dijkstra, Hans Kuyper, Greetje van der Werf, Abraham P. Buunk, and Yvonne G. van der Zee, "Social Comparison in the Classroom: A Review," *Review of Educational Research* 78, no. 4 (2008): 828–79; Dale H. Schunk and Antoinette R. Hanson, "Influence on Children's Self-Efficacy and Achievement," *Journal of Educational Psychology* 77, no. 3 (1985): 313–22.

CHAPTER TEN

1. Confucius, *The Sayings of Confucius*, trans. Leonard A. Lyall (New York: Longmans, Green, 1909).

2. Mikael Krogerus, Roman Tschäppeler, and Jenny Piening, *The Decision Book: Fifty Models for Strategic Thinking* (New York: W. W. Norton, 2012).

3. Jennifer Schriver and Nicole Teske, "Anticipating College Graduation: The Concerns and Coping Methods of College Seniors," *Journal of The First-Year Experience and Students in Transition* 32, no. 1 (2020): 79–95.

4. Graeme Drummond, "Consumer Confusion: Reduction Strategies in Higher Education," *International Journal of Educational Management* 18, no. 5 (2004): 317–23.

5. Steve Black and James D. Allen, "Part 8: Academic Help Seeking," *The Reference Librarian* 60, no. 1 (2019): 62–76; Robin Redmon Wright, "Real Men Don't Ask for Directions: Male Student Attitudes toward Peer Tutoring," *Journal of College Reading and Learning* 34, no. 1 (2003): 61–75.

6. Gail Horowitz, Laura A. Rabin, and Donald L. Brodale, "Improving Student Performance in Organic Chemistry: Help Seeking Behaviors and Prior Chemistry Aptitude," *Journal of the Scholarship of Teaching and Learning* 13, no. 3 (2013): 120–33; Stuart A. Karabenick and Myron H. Dembo, "Understanding Facilitating Self-Regulated Help Seeking," *New Directions for Teaching and Learning* 126 (2011): 33–43.

7. Jennifer Schriver and Nicole Teske, "Anticipating College Graduation: The Concerns and Coping Methods of College Seniors," *Journal of The First-Year Experience and Students in Transition* 32, no. 1 (2020): 79–95.

8. John Moyer, "A Conversation with César Chávez," *Journal of Current Social Issues* 9, no. 3 (1970).

9. Stuart A. Karabenick and Myron H. Dembo, "Understanding Facilitating Self-Regulated Help Seeking," *New Directions for Teaching and Learning* 126 (2011): 33–43.

10. Steve Black and James D. Allen, "Part 8: Academic Help Seeking," *The Reference Librarian* 60, no. 1 (2019): 62–76; Robin Redmon Wright, "Real

Men Don't Ask for Directions: Male Student Attitudes toward Peer Tutoring," *Journal of College Reading and Learning* 34, no. 1 (2003): 61–75.

CHAPTER ELEVEN

1. Thomas Jefferson, *The Works of Thomas Jefferson*, ed. Paul Leicester Ford (New York: G. P. Putnam's Sons, 1904).

2. William J. Howitz, Kate J. McKnelly, and Renee D. Link, "Developing and Implementing a Specifications Grading System in an Organic Chemistry Laboratory Course," *Journal of Chemical Education* 98, no. 2 (2021): 385–94; R. Nicholas Carleton, "Fear of the Unknown: One Fear to Rule Them All?" *Journal of Anxiety Disorders* 41 (2016): 5–21.

3. Algimantas M. Shimkunas, "Anxiety and Expectancy Change: The Effects of Failure and Uncertainty," *Journal of Personality and Social Psychology* 15, no. 1 (1970): 34–42; Michael R. Baumann, Janet A. Sniezek, Clayton A. Buerkle, "Linking Expertise and Naturalistic Decision Making," in *Linking Expertise and Naturalistic Decision Making*, ed. Eduardo Salas and Gary A. Klein (Mahwah, NJ: Lawrence Erlbaum, 2001), 139–58.

4. Stephanie A. Shields, *Speaking from the Heart: Gender and the Social Meaning of Emotion* (Cambridge: Cambridge University Press, 2002).

5. Lucius Annaeus Seneca, *Hercules Oetaeus (Hercules on Mount Oeta)*, trans. Frank Justus Miller (Morrisville, NC: Lulu Press, 2021).

6. Jeffrey S. Simons, Thomas A. Wills, Noah N. Emery, and Philip J. Spelman, "Keep Calm and Carry on: Maintaining Self-Control When Intoxicated, Upset, or Depleted," *Cognition and Emotion* 30, no. 8 (2016): 1415–29; Rebecca Abraham, "Emotional Competence as Antecedent to Performance: A Contingency Framework," *Genetic, Social, and General Psychology Monographs* 130, no. 2 (2004): 117–45.

7. John Allen Paulos, *A Mathematician Plays the Stock Market* (New York: Basic Books, 2003).

8. Tim Ferriss and Naval Ravikant, "The Tim Ferriss Show Transcripts Episode 97: Naval Ravikant," *The Tim Ferriss Show*, 2015.

9. Carol L. Flinchbaugh, E. Whitney G. Moore, Young K. Chang, and Douglas R. May, "Student Well-Being Interventions: The Effects of Stress Management Techniques and Gratitude Journaling in the Management Education Classroom," *Journal of Management Education* 36, no. 2 (2011): 191–219; Norberto Eiji Nawa and Noriko Yamagishi, "Enhanced Academic Motivation in University Students Following a 2-Week Online Gratitude Journal Intervention," *BMC Psychology* 9, no. 1 (2021): 1–16.

CHAPTER TWELVE

1. Benjamin Franklin, Henry Stevens, W. Pratt, Peter Force, Edward D. Ingraham, *Poor Richard: An Almanack, for the Year of Christ* (Philadelphia: American Almanac Collection, 1792).

2. David J. Epstein, *Range: How Generalists Triumph in a Specialized World* (New York: Macmillan, 2019).

3. Michael W. Firmin and Lisa M. MacKillop, "Frequent Major Changing: Extrinsic and Intrinsic Factors," *NACADA Journal* 28, no. 2 (2008): 5–13.

4. Barbara Hansen Lemme, *Development in Adulthood* (Saddle River, NJ: Prentice Hall, 1999).

5. Michael W. Firmin and Krista Merrick Gilson, "Driven and No Regrets: A Qualitative Analysis of Students Earning Baccalaureate Degrees in Three Years," *Educational Research Quarterly* 31, no. 2 (2007): 30–47.

6. Michael W. Firmin and Krista Merrick Gilson, "Driven and No Regrets: A Qualitative Analysis of Students Earning Baccalaureate Degrees in Three Years," *Educational Research Quarterly* 31, no. 2 (2007): 30–47.

7. Raphael D'c. Lewin, *The New Era: A Monthly Periodical Devoted to Humanity, Judaism, and Literature*, vol. 3 (London: Forgotten Books, 2019).

8. Ann Woolfolk, "Toshiko Takaezu," *Princeton Alumni Weekly* 83, no. 5 (1982): 31–33.

9. Michael C. Hollway, "A Comparison of the Impact of Two Liberal Arts General Education Core Curricula on Student Humanitarian Values," *The Journal of General Education* 54, no. 3 (2005): 237–66; Mark W. Anderson, Mario Francis Teisl, George K. Criner, Sharon Tisher, Stewart Smith, Malcolm L. Hunter, Stephen Allen Norton, Jody Jellison, Andrei Alyokhin, Eric Gallandt, Sandra Haggard, and Elizabeth Bicknell, "Attitude Changes of Undergraduate University Students in General Education Courses," *The Journal of General Education* 56, no. 2 (2007): 149–68.

10. Antonia N. Kaczkurkin and Edna B. Foa, "Cognitive-Behavioral Therapy for Anxiety Disorders: An Update on the Empirical Evidence," *Dialogues in Clinical Neuroscience* 17, no. 3 (2015): 337–46; Chelsea Moran, Christina Tomei, Monique Lefebvre, Cheryl Harris, Christine Maheu, and Sophie Lebel, "An Exploratory Study of the Worst-Case Scenario Exercise as an Exposure Treatment for Fear of Cancer Recurrence," *Supportive Care in Cancer* 25, no. 5 (2017): 1373–75; Fredrike P. Bannink, "Positive CBT: From Reducing Distress to Building Success," *Journal of Contemporary Psychotherapy* 44, no. 1 (2013): 1–8.

CHAPTER THIRTEEN

1. William Shakespeare, *Hamlet, Prince of Denmark* (Project Gutenburg, 2023), www.gutenberg.org/cache/epub/1524/pg1524

2. Arthur W. Chickering and Linda Reisser, *Education and Identity*, 2nd ed. (San Francisco: Jossey-Bass, 1993).

3. Lilach Sagiv, Sonia Roccas, Jan Cieciuch, and Shalom H. Schwartz, "Personal Values in Human Life," *Nature Human Behaviour* 1, no. 9 (2017): 630–39.

4. Andrew Miles and Catherine Yeh, "Do Demographic Predictors of Personal Values Vary by Context? A Test of Schwartz's Value Development Theory," *Social Sciences and Humanities Open* 5, no. 1 (2022): 100264.

5. Ralph Waldo Emerson, *Essays* (San Diego, CA: A Word to the Wise, 2014).

6. Michael H. Kernis and Brian M. Goldman, "A Multicomponent Conceptualization of Authenticity: Theory and Research," *Advances in Experimental Social Psychology* 38 (2006): 283–357; William E. Davis, Joshua A. Hicks, Rebecca J. Schlegel, Christina M. Smith, and Matthew Vess, "Authenticity and Self-Esteem across Temporal Horizons," *The Journal of Positive Psychology* 10, no. 2 (2014): 116–26; Francesca Gino, Maryam Kouchaki, and Adam D. Galinsky, "The Moral Virtue of Authenticity: How Inauthenticity Produces Feelings of Immorality and Impurity," *Psychological Science* 26, no. 7 (2015): 983–96.

7. Poonam Mehta, "Authenticity and Employee Wellbeing with Reference to Emotional Work: A Review," *Mental Health and Social Inclusion* 25, no. 2 (2020): 146–58; Marjo Romakkaniemi and Arja Kilpeläinen, "The Meaningful Elements in Recovering from Major Depression as a Basis of Developing Social Work in Mental Health Services," *Social Work in Mental Health* 13, no. 5 (2015): 439–58.

8. Helen M. Richardson, "Community of Values as a Factor in Friendships of College and Adult Women," *Journal of Social Psychology* 11, no. 2 (1940): 303–12.

9. Karen Gravett and Naomi E. Winstone, "Making Connections: Authenticity and Alienation within Students' Relationships in Higher Education," *Higher Education Research and Development* 41, no. 2 (2022): 360–74.

10. Rachelle Winkle-Wagner, Carmen M. McCallum, Courtney Luedke, and Brittany Ota-Malloy, "Instrumental or Meaningful Friendships: Black Alumnae Perspectives on Peer Relationships during College," *Journal of Women and Gender in Higher Education* 12, no. 3 (2019): 283–98.

11. Francesca Gino, Maryam Kouchaki, and Adam D. Galinsky, "The Moral Virtue of Authenticity: How Inauthenticity Produces Feelings of Immorality and Impurity," *Psychological Science* 26, no. 7 (2015): 983–96.

12. Güler Boyraz, J. Brandon Waits, and Victoria A. Felix, "Authenticity, Life Satisfaction, and Distress: A Longitudinal Analysis," *Journal of Counseling Psychology* 61, no. 3 (2014): 498–505.

13. Francesca Gino, Maryam Kouchaki, and Adam D. Galinsky, "The Moral Virtue of Authenticity: How Inauthenticity Produces Feelings of Immorality and Impurity," *Psychological Science* 26, no. 7 (2015): 983–96.

14. Michael H. Kernis and Brian M. Goldman, "A Multicomponent Conceptualization of Authenticity: Theory and Research," *Advances in Experimental Social Psychology* 38 (2006): 283–357; William E. Davis, Joshua A. Hicks, Rebecca J. Schlegel, Christina M. Smith, and Matthew Vess, "Authenticity and Self-Esteem across Temporal Horizons," *The Journal of Positive Psychology* 10, no. 2 (2014): 116–26; Francesca Gino, Maryam Kouchaki, and Adam D. Galinsky, "The Moral Virtue of Authenticity: How Inauthenticity Produces Feelings of Immorality and Impurity," *Psychological Science* 26, no. 7 (2015): 983–96.

15. Christopher J. Hopwood, Evan W. Good, Alytia A. Levendosky, Johannes Zimmermann, Daniela Dumat, Eli J. Finkel, Paul E. Eastwick, and Wiebke Bleidorn, "Realness Is a Core Feature of Authenticity," *Journal of Research in Personality* 92 (2021): 104086.

16. William E. Davis, Joshua A. Hicks, Rebecca J. Schlegel, Christina M. Smith, and Matthew Vess, "Authenticity and Self-Esteem across Temporal Horizons," *The Journal of Positive Psychology* 10, no. 2 (2014): 116–26; Christopher J. Hopwood, Evan W. Good, Alytia A. Levendosky, Johannes Zimmermann, Daniela Dumat, Eli J. Finkel, Paul E. Eastwick, and Wiebke Bleidorn, "Realness Is a Core Feature of Authenticity," *Journal of Research in Personality* 92 (2021): 104086.

17. Carl Ransom Rogers, *On Becoming a Person: A Therapist's View of Psychotherapy* (San Francisco: HarperOne, 1995).

CHAPTER FOURTEEN

1. Benjamin Franklin, Henry Stevens, W. Pratt, Peter Force, Edward D. Ingraham, American Almanac Collection, and Marian S. Carson Collection, *Poor Richard: An Almanack, for the Year of Christ* (Philadelphia: Printed and sold by B. Franklin, 1758), www.loc.gov/item/2001204984/.

2. Mary P. Quayhagen and Margaret Quayhagen, "Alzheimer's Stress: Coping with the Caregiving Role," *The Gerontologist* 28, no. 3 (1988): 391–96.

3. Olya Bullard and Rajesh V. Manchanda, "How Goal Progress Influences Regulatory Focus in Goal Pursuit," *Journal of Consumer Psychology* 27, no. 3 (2017): 302–17.

4. Carol E. Ford and Jack W. Brehm, "Effort Expenditure Following Failure," in *Coping with Negative Life Events: The Plenum Series on Stress and Coping*, ed. C. R. Snyder and C. E. Ford (Boston: Springer, 1987), 81–103.

5. Roy F. Baumeister and John Tierney, *Willpower: Rediscovering the Greatest Human Strength* (New York: Penguin, 2011).

6. Cor J. M. Suhre, Ellen P. W. A. Jansen, and Egbert G. Harskamp, "Impact of Degree Program Satisfaction on the Persistence of College Students," *Higher Education* 54, no. 2 (2006): 207–26.

7. Maureen Snow Andrade, Ronald Mellado Miller, David McArthur, and Morgan Ogden, "The Impact of Learning on Student Persistence in Higher Education," *Journal of College Student Retention: Research, Theory and Practice* 24, no. 2 (2022): 316–36; Victor M. H. Borden, "Segmenting Student Markets with a Student Satisfaction and Priorities Survey," *Research in Higher Education* 36, no. 1 (1995): 73–88.

8. Dale H. Schunk and Barry J. Zimmerman, *Self-Regulation of Learning and Performance: Issues and Educational Applications* (Mahwah, NJ: Lawrence Erlbaum, 1994); Elizabeth J. Krumrei-Mancuso, Fred B. Newton, Eunhee Kim, and Dan Wilcox, "Psychosocial Factors Predicting First-Year College Student Success," *Journal of College Student Development* 54, no. 3 (2013): 247–66.

9. "On the Shortness of Life," trans. John W. Basore (London: William Heinemann, 1932).

10. Dale H. Schunk, "Goal Setting and Self-Efficacy during Self-Regulated Learning," *Educational Psychologist* 25, no. 1 (1990): 71–86; Olya Bullard and Rajesh V. Manchanda, "How Goal Progress Influences Regulatory Focus in Goal Pursuit," *Journal of Consumer Psychology* 27, no. 3 (2017): 302–17.

11. Peter A. Cohen, James A. Kulik, and Chen-Lin C. Kulik, "Educational Outcomes of Tutoring: A Meta-Analysis of Findings," *American Educational Research Journal* 19, no. 2 (1982): 237–48; Maria G. Valdovinos, "The Impact of a Year-Long Service-Learning Experience on Student Perception of Ability to Conduct Functional Assessments," *Scholarship of Teaching and Learning in Psychology* 2, no. 2 (2016): 125–33; Jeffrey Scott Coker, Evan Heiser, Laura Taylor, and Connie Book, "Impacts of Experiential Learning Depth and Breadth on Student Outcomes," *Journal of Experiential Education* 40, no. 1 (2016): 5–23.

12. Sonja Lyubomirsky, Laura King, and Ed Diener, "The Benefits of Frequent Positive Affect: Does Happiness Lead to Success?" *Psychological Bulletin* 131, no. 6 (2005): 803–55.

CHAPTER FIFTEEN

1. Lucius Annaeus Seneca, *Moral Letters to Lucilius—Letters from a Stoic*, trans. Richard M. Gummere (Cambridge, MA: Loeb Classical Library Edition, 1915).

2. Nicolas Roulin and Adrian Bangerter, "Extracurricular Activities in Young Applicants' Résumés: What Are the Motives behind Their Involvement?" *International Journal of Psychology* 48, no. 5 (2013): 871–80.

3. Amanda C. Weldy Boyd, "I Came, I Saw, I Put It on My Resume for Medical School," *Journal of College and Character* 12, no. 4 (2011); Constance Flanagan and Matthew Bundick, "Civic Engagement and Psychosocial Well-Being in College Students," *Liberal Education* 97, no. 2 (2011): 20–27; Thanh-Thanh Tieu and S. Mark Pancer, "Cocurricular Involvement and First-Year Students' Transition to University: Quality vs. Quantity of Involvement," *Journal of The First-Year Experience and Students in Transition* 21, no. 1 (2009): 43–63.

4. Nicolas Roulin and Adrian Bangerter, "Extracurricular Activities in Young Applicants' Résumés: What Are the Motives behind Their Involvement?" *International Journal of Psychology* 48, no. 5 (2013): 871–80; Amanda C. Weldy Boyd, "I Came, I Saw, I Put It on My Resume for Medical School," *Journal of College and Character* 12, no. 4 (2011).

5. Michael S. Cole, Robert S. Rubin, Hubert S. Feild, and William F. Giles, "Recruiters' Perceptions and Use of Applicant Résumé Information: Screening the Recent Graduate," *Applied Psychology* 56, no. 2 (2007): 319–43.

6. Michael S. Cole, Robert S. Rubin, Hubert S. Feild, and William F. Giles, "Recruiters' Perceptions and Use of Applicant Résumé Information: Screening the Recent Graduate," *Applied Psychology* 56, no. 2 (2007): 319–43.

7. Amanda C. Weldy Boyd, "I Came, I Saw, I Put It on My Resume for Medical School," *Journal of College and Character* 12, no. 4 (2011).

8. Jesse Owens and Paul G. Neimark, *Jesse, a Spiritual Autobiography* (Plainfield, NJ: Logos International, 1978).

9. Kristin M. Vespia, Georjeanna Wilson-Doenges, Ryan C. Martin, and Deirdre M. Radosevich, "Experiential Learning," in *Evidence-Based Teaching for Higher Education*, ed. B. M. Schwartz and R. A. R. Gurung (Washington, DC: American Psychological Association, 2012), 97.

10. Kristin M. Vespia, Georjeanna Wilson-Doenges, Ryan C. Martin, and Deirdre M. Radosevich, "Experiential Learning," in *Evidence-Based Teaching for Higher Education*, ed. B. M. Schwartz and R. A. R. Gurung (Washington, DC: American Psychological Association, 2012), 97; Jack Russell, Barbara Russell, and William J. Tastle, "Teaching Soft Skills in a Systems Development Capstone Class," *Information Systems Education Journal* 3, no. 19 (2005).

11. Kristin M. Vespia, Georjeanna Wilson-Doenges, Ryan C. Martin, and Deirdre M. Radosevich, "Experiential Learning," in *Evidence-Based Teaching for Higher Education*, ed. B. M. Schwartz and R. A. R. Gurung (Washington, DC: American Psychological Association, 2012), 97; Jack Russell, Barbara Russell, and William J. Tastle, "Teaching Soft Skills in a Systems Development Capstone Class," *Information Systems Education Journal* 3, no. 19 (2005).

CHAPTER SIXTEEN

1. Plato, *Gorgias*, trans. Benjamin Jowett (Project Gutenberg, 2022), www.gutenberg.org/files/1672/1672-h/1672-h.htm.

2. Ani Yazedjian, Becki Kielaszek, and Michelle Toews, "Students' Perceptions Regarding Their Impending Transition out of College," *Journal of The First-Year Experience and Students in Transition* 22, no. 2 (2010): 33–48; Blake R. Silver and Josipa Roksa, "Navigating Uncertainty and Responsibility: Understanding Inequality in the Senior-Year Transition," *Journal of Student Affairs Research and Practice* 54, no. 3 (2017): 248–60.

3. Joshua Wilt, Wiebke Bleidorn, and William Revelle, "Finding a Life Worth Living: Meaning in Life and Graduation from College," *European Journal of Personality* 30, no. 2 (2016): 158–67.

4. Ani Yazedjian, Becki Kielaszek, and Michelle Toews, "Students' Perceptions Regarding Their Impending Transition out of College," *Journal of The First-Year Experience and Students in Transition* 22, no. 2 (2010): 33–48; Blake R. Silver and Josipa Roksa, "Navigating Uncertainty and Responsibility: Understanding Inequality in the Senior-Year Transition," *Journal of Student Affairs Research and Practice* 54, no. 3 (2017): 248–60.

5. Dalai Lama, *The Dalai Lama's Little Book of Inner Peace: The Essential Life and Teachings* (Newburyport, MA: Hampton Roads, 2009).

6. Marcus Aurelius, *Meditations*, trans. Robin Hard (New York: Oxford University Press, 2011).

7. Ani Yazedjian, Becki Kielaszek, and Michelle Toews, "Students' Perceptions Regarding Their Impending Transition out of College," *Journal of

The First-Year Experience and Students in Transition 22, no. 2 (2010): 33–48; Blake R. Silver and Josipa Roksa, "Navigating Uncertainty and Responsibility: Understanding Inequality in the Senior-Year Transition," *Journal of Student Affairs Research and Practice* 54, no. 3 (2017): 248–60.

8. Thomas R. Hensley, Kathleen Hale, and Carl Snook, *The Rehnquist Court: Justices, Rulings, and Legacy* (Santa Barbara, CA: ABC-CLIO, 2006).

9. Miriam Rothman and Ruth Sisman, "Internship Impact on Career Consideration among Business Students," *Education and Training* 58, no. 9 (2016): 1003–13; Alexandra M. Schnoes, Anne Caliendo, Janice Morand, Teresa Dillinger, Michelle Naffziger-Hirsch, Bruce Moses, Jeffery C. Gibeling, Keith R. Yamamoto, Bill Lindstaedt, Richard McGee, and Theresa C. O'Brien, "Internship Experiences Contribute to Confident Career Decision Making for Doctoral Students in the Life Sciences," *CBE Life Sciences Education* 17, no. 1 (2018): ar16.

10. J. R. R. Tolkien, *The Fellowship of the Ring: Being the First Part of The Lord of the Rings* (New York: Ballantine Books, 1997).

11. Melita Puklek Levpušček, Victoria Rauch, and Luka Komidar, "Individuation in Relation to Parents as a Predictor of Career Goals and Career Optimism in Emerging Adults," *Scandinavian Journal of Psychology* 59, no. 2 (2018): 146–56; Madonna G. Constantine and Lisa Y. Flores, "Psychological Distress, Perceived Family Conflict, and Career Development Issues in College Students of Color," *Journal of Career Assessment* 14, no. 3 (2006): 354–69.

12. J. Michael Bishop and Harold E. Varmus, "Harold E. Varmus—Biographical," *Nobel Prize Outreach*, 1989, www.nobelprize.org/prizes/medicine/1989/varmus/biographical/ (accessed February 13, 2020).

13. Ashley Stahl, "Six Reasons Why Your College Major Doesn't Matter," *Forbes*, 2015, www.forbes.Com/Sites/Ashleystahl/2015/08/12/Six-Reasons-Why-Your-College-Major-Doesnt-Matter/?Sh=66300a8e35a0 (accessed February 20, 2020); Jaison R. Abel and Richard Deitz, "Do Big Cities Help College Graduates Find Better Jobs?" Liberty Street Economics, May 20, 2013, https://libertystreeteconomics.newyorkfed.org/2013/05/do-big-cities-help-college-graduates-find-better-jobs (accessed March 3, 2020).

14. Ashley Stahl, "Six Reasons Why Your College Major Doesn't Matter," *Forbes*, August 12, 2015, www.forbes.Com/Sites/Ashleystahl/2015/08/12/Six-Reasons-Why-Your-College-Major-Doesnt-Matter/?Sh=66300a8e35a0 (accessed February 20, 2020).

15. "U.S. Census Bureau Releases New Educational Attainment Data," U.S. Census, 2020.

EPILOGUE

1. Epictetus, *Discourses, Fragments, Handbook*, trans. Robin Hard (New York: Oxford World's Classics, 2014).
2. Marcus Aurelius, *Meditations*, trans. Robin Hard (New York: Oxford University Press, 2011).
3. Lucius Annaeus Seneca, *Letters on Ethics: To Lucilius*, trans. Margaret Graver and A. A. Long (Chicago: University of Chicago Press, 2015); Lucius Annaeus Seneca, *Anger, Mercy, Revenge—The Complete Works of Lucius Annaeus Seneca*, trans. Robert A. Kaster and Martha C. Nussbaum (Chicago: University of Chicago Press, 2010); Lucius Annaeus Seneca, *Hardship and Happiness*, trans. Elaine Fathom, Harry M. Hine, James Ker, and Gareth D. Williams (Chicago: University of Chicago Press, 2016).
4. Lucius Annaeus Seneca, *Letters from a Stoic*, trans. Coralie Bickford-Smith and Robin Campbell (London: Penguin Classics, 2015); Lucius Annaeus Seneca, *Letters on Ethics: To Lucilius*, trans. Margaret Graver and A. A. Long (Chicago: University of Chicago Press, 2015).
5. Massimo Pigliucci and Gregory Lopez, *A Handbook for New Stoics: How to Thrive in a World out of Your Control: 52 Week-by-Week Lessons* (New York: The Experiment, 2019).
6. Donald Robertson, *How to Think Like a Roman Emperor: The Stoic Philosophy of Marcus Aurelius* (New York: St. Martin's, 2019).
7. William Irvine, *A Guide to the Good Life: The Ancient Art of Stoic Joy* (New York: Oxford University Press, 2008).
8. Ryan Holiday, *The Obstacle Is the Way: The Ancient Art of Turning Adversity to Advantage* (London: Profile Books, 2014); Ryan Holiday, *Ego Is the Enemy* (New York: Portfolio, 2016).
9. Martin E. P. Seligman, *Authentic Happiness: Using the New Positive Psychology to Realize Your Potential for Lasting Fulfillment* (New York: Free Press, 2002).
10. Angela Duckworth *Grit: The Power of Passion and Perseverance* (New York: Scribner, 2016).

APPENDIX

1. Amy Wrzesniewski, Barry Schwartz, Xiangyu Cong, Michael Kane, Audrey Omar, and Thomas Kolditz, "Multiple Types of Motives Don't Multiply the Motivation of West Point Cadets," *Proceedings of the National Academy of Sciences of the United States of America* 111, no. 30 (2014): 10990–95; Naomi

Noel Trevino and Stacie Craft DeFreitas, "The Relationship between Intrinsic Motivation and Academic Achievement for First Generation Latino College Students," *Social Psychology of Education* 17, no. 2 (2014): 293–306; Joke Simons, Siegfried Dewitte, and Willy Lens, "The Role of Different Types of Instrumentality in Motivation, Study Strategies, and Performance: Know Why You Learn, So You'll Know What You Learn!" *British Journal of Educational Psychology* 74, no. 3 (2004): 343–60; Judith M. Harackiewicz, Kenneth E. Barron, and Andrew J. Elliot, "Rethinking Achievement Goals: When Are They Adaptive for College Students and Why?" *Educational Psychologist* 33, no. 1 (1998): 1–21; John Mark Froiland, Emily Oros, Liana Smith, and Tyrell Hirchert, "Intrinsic Motivation to Learn: The Nexus between Psychological Health and Academic Succes," *Contemporary School Psychology* 16, no. 1 (2014): 91–100.

BIBLIOGRAPHY

Abel, Jaison R., and Richard Deitz. "Do Big Cities Help College Graduates Find Better Jobs?" Liberty Street Economics. May 20, 2013. https://libertystreeteconomics.newyorkfed.org/.

Abraham, Rebecca. "Emotional Competence as Antecedent to Performance: A Contingency Framework." *Genetic, Social, and General Psychology Monographs* 130, no. 2 (2004): 117–45. https://doi.org/10.3200/MONO.130.2.117-145.

Acaster, James. "Mock the Week—Series 15, Episode 11." United Kingdom, n.d. Accessed March 29, 2022.

Adil, Adnan, Sadaf Ameer, and Saba Ghayas. "Impact of Academic Psychological Capital on Academic Achievement among University Undergraduates: Roles of Flow and Self-Handicapping Behavior." *PsyCh Journal* 9, no. 1 (2020): 56–66. https://doi.org/10.1002/PCHJ.318.

Aesop. *Aesop's Fables: A New Translation*. Translated by V. S. Vernon Stanley Jones. Dodo Press, 2009.

Ahuvia, Aaron. "If Money Doesn't Make Us Happy, Why Do We Act as If It Does?" *Journal of Economic Psychology* 29, no. 4 (2008): 491–507. https://doi.org/10.1016/J.JOEP.2007.11.005.

Anderson, Mark W., Mario Francis Teisl, George K. Criner, Sharon Tisher, Stewart Smith, Malcolm L. Hunter, Stephen Allen Norton, Jody Jellison, Andrei Alyokhin, Eric Gallandt, Sandra Haggard, and Elizabeth Bicknell. "Attitude Changes of Undergraduate University Students in General Education Courses." *The Journal of General Education* 56, no. 2 (2007): 149–68. https://doi.org/10.1353/JGE.2007.0016.

Andrade, Maureen Snow, Ronald Mellado Miller, David McArthur, and Morgan Ogden. "The Impact of Learning on Student Persistence in Higher Education." *Journal of College Student Retention: Research, Theory and Practice* 24, no. 2 (2022): 316–36. https://doi.org/10.1177/1521025120915576.

Aristotle. *Nicomachean Ethics*. Edited by Terence Irwin. 2nd ed. Indianapolis: Hackett, 1999.

Banksy. *Cut It Out*. Chico, CA: AKPress, 2004.

Bannink, F. P. "Positive CBT: From Reducing Distress to Building Success." *Journal of Contemporary Psychotherapy* 44, no. 1 (2013): 1–8. https://doi.org/10.1007/S10879-013-9239-7.

Baumann, M. R., J. A. Sniezek, and C. A. Buerkle. "Linking Expertise and Naturalistic Decision Making." In *Linking Expertise and Naturalistic Decision Making*, edited by E. Salas and G. Klein, 139–58. Mahwah, NJ: Lawrence Erlbaum, 2001. https://doi.org/10.4324/9781410604200.

Baumeister, Roy F., and John Tierney. *Willpower: Rediscovering the Greatest Human Strength*. New York: Penguin Press, 2011.

Baumeister, Roy F., and Kathleen D. Vohs. "Narcissism as Addiction to Esteem." *Psychological Inquiry* 12, no. 4 (2001): 206–10.

Belapurkar, Anita H. G. M. "Understanding Self and Its Importance in Education." *Scholarly Research Journal for Interdisciplinary Studies* 4, no. 25 (2016): 2433–39.

Bellezza, Silvia, Neeru Paharia, and Anat Keinan. "Conspicuous Consumption of Time: When Busyness and Lack of Leisure Time Become a Status Symbol." *Journal of Consumer Research* 44, no. 1 (2017): 118–38. https://doi.org/10.1093/jcr/ucw076.

Bishop, J. Michael, and Harold E. Varmus. "Harold E. Varmus—Biographical." *Nobel Prize Outreach*, 1989. www.nobelprize.org/prizes/medicine/1989/varmus/biographical/.

Black, Paul, and Dylan Wiliam. "Assessment and Classroom Learning." *Assessment in Education: Principles, Policy and Practice* 21, no. 1 (1998): 7–74. https://doi.org/10.1080/0969595980050102.

Black, Steve, and James D. Allen. "Part 8: Academic Help Seeking." *The Reference Librarian* 60, no. 1 (2019): 62–76. https://doi.org/10.1080/02763877.2018.1533910.

Borden, Victor M. H. "Segmenting Student Markets with a Student Satisfaction and Priorities Survey." *Research in Higher Education* 36, no. 1 (1995): 73–88. https://doi.org/10.1007/BF02207767.

Boyd, Amanda C. Weldy. "I Came, I Saw, I Put It on My Resume for Medical School." *Journal of College and Character* 12, no. 4 (2011). https://doi.org/10.2202/1940-1639.1854.

Boyraz, Güler, J. Brandon Waits, and Victoria A. Felix. "Authenticity, Life Satisfaction, and Distress: A Longitudinal Analysis." *Journal of Counseling Psychology* 61, no. 3 (2014): 498–505. https://doi.org/10.1037/COU0000031.

Broh, Beckett A. "Linking Extracurricular Programming to Academic Achievement: Who Benefits and Why?" *Sociology of Education* 75, no. 1 (2002): 69–95. https://doi.org/10.2307/3090254.

Brown, Brené. *Rising Strong*. New York: Random House, 2015.

Budnick, Christopher J., Arielle P. Rogers, and Larissa K. Barber. "The Fear of Missing out at Work: Examining Costs and Benefits to Employee Health and Motivation." *Computers in Human Behavior* 104 (2020): 106161. https://doi.org/10.1016/J.CHB.2019.106161.

Bullard, Olya, and Rajesh v. Manchanda. "How Goal Progress Influences Regulatory Focus in Goal Pursuit." *Journal of Consumer Psychology* 27, no. 3 (2017): 302–17. https://doi.org/10.1016/J.JCPS.2017.01.003.

Burke, Peter J. "The Self: Measurement Requirements from an Interactionist Perspective." *Social Psychology Quarterly* 43, no. 1 (1980): 18. https://doi.org/10.2307/3033745.

Bushman, Brad J., Scott J. Moeller, and Jennifer Crocker. "Sweets, Sex, or Self-Esteem? Comparing the Value of Self-Esteem Boosts with Other Pleasant Rewards." *Journal of Personality* 79, no. 5 (2011): 993–1012. https://doi.org/10.1111/J.1467-6494.2011.00712.X.

Calvo, Manuel G., and Michael W. Eysenck. "Anxiety and Performance: The Processing Efficiency Theory." *Cognition and Emotion* 6, no. 6 (1992): 409–34. https://doi.org/10.1080/02699939208409696.

Camp, William G. "Participation in Student Activities and Achievement: A Covariance Structural Analysis." *The Journal of Educational Research* 83, no. 5 (1990): 271–78. https://doi.org/10.1080/00220671.1990.10885969.

Campbell, Ernest T. "What's the Story?" *Ernest T. Campbell Manuscript Collection*. Box 4, no. 28 (1973).

Campbell, Joseph. *The Hero's Journey: Joseph Campbell on His Life and Work*. Edited by Phil Cousineau. San Francisco: Harper San Francisco, 1991.

Campion, Michael A., and Robert G. Lord. "A Control Systems Conceptualization of the Goal-Setting and Changing Process." *Organizational Behavior and Human Performance* 30, no. 2 (1982): 265–87. https://doi.org/10.1016/0030-5073(82)90221-5.

Carden, Randy, Courtney Bryant, and Rebekah Moss. "Locus of Control, Test Anxiety, Academic Procrastination, and Achievement among College Students." *Psychological Reports* 95, no. 2 (2004): 581–82. https://doi.org/10.2466/PR0.95.2.581-582.

Carleton, R. Nicholas. "Fear of the Unknown: One Fear to Rule Them All?" *Journal of Anxiety Disorders* 41 (2016): 5–21. https://doi.org/10.1016/J.JANXDIS.2016.03.011.

Cervantes Saavedra, Miguel de. *The Ingenious Hidalgo Don Quixote de La Mancha*. Translated by John Rutherford. New York: Penguin Classics, 2003.

Chickering, Arthur W., and Linda Reisser. *Education and Identity*. 2nd ed. San Francisco: Jossey-Bass, 1993.

Christian Commission for Camp and Defense Communities. *A Book of Prayers for the Armed Forces by Commission on Worship of the Federal Council of the Churches of Christ in America*. White/Walnut Valley Books, 1944.

Christopher, Andrew N., Terell P. Lasane, Jordan D. Troisi, and Lora E. Park. "Materialism, Defensive and Assertive Self-Presentational Tactics, and Life Satisfaction." *Journal of Social and Clinical Psychology* 26, no. 10 (2007): 1145–62. https://doi.org/10.1521/JSCP.2007.26.10.1145.

Christopher, Andrew N., Liliane Saliba, and Erik J. Deadmarsh. "Materialism and Well-Being: The Mediating Effect of Locus of Control." *Personality and Individual Differences* 46, no. 7 (2009): 682–86. https://doi.org/10.1016/J.PAID.2009.01.003.

Cohen, Peter A., James A. Kulik, and Chen-Lin C. Kulik. "Educational Outcomes of Tutoring: A Meta-Analysis of Findings." *American Educational Research Journal* 19, no. 2 (1982): 237–48. https://doi.org/10.3102/00028312019002237.

Coker, Jeffrey Scott, Evan Heiser, Laura Taylor, and Connie Book. "Impacts of Experiential Learning Depth and Breadth on Student Outcomes." *Journal of Experiential Education* 40, no. 1 (2016): 5–23. https://doi.org/10.1177/1053825916678265.

Cole, Michael S., Robert S. Rubin, Hubert S. Feild, and William F. Giles. "Recruiters' Perceptions and Use of Applicant Résumé Information: Screening the Recent Graduate." *Applied Psychology* 56, no. 2 (2007): 319–43. https://doi.org/10.1111/J.1464-0597.2007.00288.X.

Confucius. *The Sayings of Confucius*. Translated by James R. Ware. New York: New American Library, 1955.

Congreve, William, J. Thornthwaite, and James Roberts. *The Mourning Bride*. Wentworth Press, 2019.

Constantine, Madonna G., and Lisa Y. Flores. "Psychological Distress, Perceived Family Conflict, and Career Development Issues in College Students of Color." *Journal of Career Assessment* 14, no. 3 (2006): 354–69. https://doi.org/10.1177/1069072706286491.

Crocker, C. G. "Frankford." *Delmarva News*, December 7, 1967.

Cross, Ainslea, and David Sheffield. "Mental Contrasting as a Behaviour Change Technique: A Systematic Review Protocol Paper of Effects,

Mediators and Moderators on Health." *Systematic Reviews* 5, no. 1 (2016): 1–6. https://doi.org/10.1186/S13643-016-0382-6/TABLES/1.

Cutrona, C. E. "Transition to College: Loneliness and the Process of Social Adjustment." In *Loneliness: A Sourcebook of Current Theory, Research and Practice*, edited by L. A. Peplau and D. Pearlman, 291–309. New York: Wiley Interscience, 1982.

Dalai Lama. *The Dalai Lama's Little Book of Inner Peace: The Essential Life and Teachings*. Hampton Roads Publishing, 2009.

Dante Alighieri. *The Divine Comedy: The Inferno, the Purgatorio, and the Paradiso*. Translated by John Ciardi. New York: New American Library, 2003.

Davis, William E., Joshua A. Hicks, Rebecca J. Schlegel, Christina M. Smith, and Matthew Vess. "Authenticity and Self-Esteem across Temporal Horizons." *The Journal of Positive Psychology* 10, no. 2 (2014): 116–26. https://doi.org/10.1080/17439760.2014.910830.

D'c. Lewin, Raphael. *The New Era: A Monthly Periodical Devoted to Humanity, Judaism, and Literature*. Vol. 3. London: Forgotten Books, 2019.

Deci, Edward L. *Intrinsic Motivation*. New York: Plenum Press, 1975.

Depreeuw, Eric, and Hubert de Neve. "Test Anxiety Can Harm Your Health: Some Conclusions Based on a Student Typology." In *Anxiety: Recent Developments in Cognitive, Psychophysiological, and Health Research*, edited by Donald G. Forgays, Tytus Sosnowski, and Kazimierz Wrzesniewski, 211–28. New York: Taylor & Francis, 1992. https://doi.org/10.4324/9781315825199-16.

Dijkstra, Pieternel, Hans Kuyper, Greetje van der Werf, Abraham P. Buunk, and Yvonne G. van der Zee. "Social Comparison in the Classroom: A Review," *Review of Educational Research* 78, no. 4 (2008): 828–79. https://doi.org/10.3102/0034654308321210.

Docter, Pete, and Amy Poehler. *The Art of Inside Out*. San Francisco: Chronicle Books, 2015.

Dolan, Paul, Tessa Peasgood, and Mathew White. "Do We Really Know What Makes Us Happy? A Review of the Economic Literature on the Factors Associated with Subjective Well-Being." *Journal of Economic Psychology* 29, no. 1 (2008): 94–122. https://doi.org/10.1016/J.JOEP.2007.09.001.

Drew, Susan, and Ruth Paradice. "Time, Women and Well-Being." *Feminism and Psychology* 6, no. 4 (1996): 563–68.

Drummond, Graeme. "Consumer Confusion: Reduction Strategies in Higher Education." *International Journal of Educational Management* 18, no.

5 (2004): 317–23. https://doi.org/10.1108/09513540410543466/FULL/PDF.

Duckworth, Angela. *Grit: The Power of Passion and Perseverance.* New York: Scribner, 2016.

Dyer, Wayne W. "If You Are Always in a Hurry." Facebook, March 24, 2015. www.facebook.com/drwaynedyer/posts/10153158629826030.

Earhart, Amelia. The Official Licensing Website of Amelia Earhart. n.d. www.ameliaearhart.com/Quotes.

Emerson, Ralph Waldo. *Essays.* A Word to the Wise, 2014.

Epictetus. *Discourses, Fragments, Handbook.* Translated by Robin Hard. New York: Oxford World Classics, 2014.

Epstein, David J. *Range: How Generalists Triumph in a Specialized World.* New York: Macmillan, 2019.

Ferrari, Joseph R. "Self-Handicapping by Procrastinators: Protecting Self-Esteem, Social-Esteem, or Both?" *Journal of Research in Personality* 25, no. 3 (1991): 245–61. https://doi.org/10.1016/0092-6566(91)90018-L.

Ferriss, Tim, and Naval Ravikant. "The Tim Ferriss Show Transcripts Episode 97: Naval Ravikant." *The Tim Ferriss Show,* 2015.

Ferriss, Timothy. *The 4-Hour Workweek: Escape 9-5, Live Anywhere, and Join the New Rich.* New York: Crown Publishers, 2007.

Findley, Maureen J., and Harris M. Cooper. "Locus of Control and Academic Achievement: A Literature Review." *Journal of Personality and Social Psychology* 44, no. 2 (1983): 419–27. https://doi.org/10.1037/0022-3514.44.2.419.

Finucane, Anne M. "The Effect of Fear and Anger on Selective Attention." *Emotion* 11, no. 4 (2011): 970–74. https://doi.org/10.1037/A0022574.

Firmin, Michael W., and Krista Merrick Gilson. "Driven and No Regrets: A Qualitative Analysis of Students Earning Baccalaureate Degrees in Three Years." *Educational Research Quarterly* 31, no. 2 (2007): 30–47.

Firmin, Michael W., and Lisa M. MacKillop. "Frequent Major Changing: Extrinsic and Intrinsic Factors." *NACADA Journal* 28, no. 2 (2008): 5–13. https://doi.org/10.12930/0271-9517-28.2.5.

Flanagan, Constance, and Matthew Bundick. "Civic Engagement and Psychosocial Well-Being in College Students." *Liberal Education* 97, no. 2 (2011): 20–27.

Flinchbaugh, Carol L., E. Whitney G. Moore, Young K. Chang, and Douglas R. May. "Student Well-Being Interventions: The Effects of Stress Management Techniques and Gratitude Journaling in the Management Education Classroom." *Journal of Management Education* 36, no. 2 (2011): 191–219. https://doi.org/10.1177/1052562911430062.

Ford, Carol E., and Jack W. Brehm. "Effort Expenditure Following Failure." In *Coping with Negative Life Events: The Plenum Series on Stress and Coping*, edited by C. R. Snyder and C. E. Ford, 81–103. Boston: Springer, 1987. https://doi.org/10.1007/978-1-4757-9865-4_4.

Foulsham, Tom, Rana Alan, and Alan Kingstone. "Scrambled Eyes? Disrupting Scene Structure Impedes Focal Processing and Increases Bottom-up Guidance." *Attention, Perception, and Psychophysics* 73, no. 7 (2011): 2008–25. https://doi.org/10.3758/S13414-011-0158-Y/FIGURES/6.

Franklin, Benjamin. *Poor Richard's Almanack*. Peter Pauper Press, 1988.

Froiland, John Mark, Emily Oros, Liana Smith, and Tyrell Hirchert. "Intrinsic Motivation to Learn: The Nexus between Psychological Health and Academic Success." *Contemporary School Psychology* 16, no. 1 (2014): 91–100. https://doi.org/10.1007/BF03340978.

Frost, Robert. *The Road Not Taken*. Illustrated by Vivian Mineker. Familius, 2019.

Garner, Bryan A. "Cultivate the Right Demeanor for Effective Legal Writing." *Michigan Bar Journal*, February 2010.

Gass, Kathleen A., and Audrey S. Chang. "Appraisals of Bereavement, Coping, Resources, and Psychosocial Health Dysfunction in Widows and Widowers." *Nursing Research* 38, no. 1 (1989): 31–36.

Gino, Francesca, Maryam Kouchaki, and Adam D. Galinsky. "The Moral Virtue of Authenticity: How Inauthenticity Produces Feelings of Immorality and Impurity." *Psychological Science* 26, no. 7 (2015): 983–96. https://doi.org/10.1177/0956797615575277.

Goffman, E. *The Presentation of Self in Everyday Life*. Garden City, NY: Doubleday, 1959.

Goldthwait, Bobcat. *World's Greatest Dad*. Magnolia Pictures, 2009.

Gravett, Karen, and Naomi E. Winstone. "Making Connections: Authenticity and Alienation within Students' Relationships in Higher Education." *Higher Education Research & Development* 41, no. 2 (2022): 360–74. https://doi.org/10.1080/07294360.2020.1842335.

Hamm, Robert. "Negative Will, Self-Image, and Personality Dysfunction." *Psychoanalytic Review* 96, no. 1 (2009): 55–82. https://doi.org/10.1521/prev.2009.96.1.55.

Harackiewicz, Judith M., Kenneth E. Barron, and Andrew J. Elliot. "Rethinking Achievement Goals: When Are They Adaptive for College Students and Why?" *Educational Psychologist* 33, no. 1 (1998): 1–21. https://doi.org/10.1207/S15326985EP3301_1.

Harter, S. "The Development of Self-Representations." In *Handbook of Child Psychology: Social, Emotional, and Personality Development*, edited by

W. Damon and N. Eisenberg, 553–617. Hoboken, NJ: John Wiley & Sons, 1998.

Hawkley, Louise C., and John T. Cacioppo. "Loneliness Matters: A Theoretical and Empirical Review of Consequences and Mechanisms." *Annals of Behavioral Medicine: A Publication of the Society of Behavioral Medicine* 40, no. 2 (2010): 218–27. https://doi.org/10.1007/S12160-010-9210-8.

Hawkley, Louise C., and John P. Capitanio. "Perceived Social Isolation, Evolutionary Fitness and Health Outcomes: A Lifespan Approach." *Philosophical Transactions of the Royal Society B: Biological Sciences* 370, no. 1669 (May 26, 2015). https://doi.org/10.1098/RSTB.2014.0114.

Heinrich, Liesl M., and Eleonora Gullone. "The Clinical Significance of Loneliness: A Literature Review." *Clinical Psychology Review* 26, no. 6 (2006): 695–718. https://doi.org/10.1016/J.CPR.2006.04.002.

Hensley, Thomas R., Kathleen Hale, and Carl Snook. *The Rehnquist Court: Justices, Rulings, and Legacy.* Santa Barbara, CA: ABC-CLIO, 2006.

Hillesum, Etty, K. A. D. Smelik, and Arnold Pomerans. *Etty: The Letters and Diaries of Etty Hillesum, 1941–1943.* Grand Rapids, MI: William B. Eerdmans, 2002.

Holiday, Ryan. *Ego Is the Enemy.* Portfolio, 2016.

———. *The Obstacle Is the Way: The Ancient Art of Turning Adversity to Advantage.* Profile Books, 2014.

Hollway, Michael C. "A Comparison of the Impact of Two Liberal Arts General Education Core Curricula on Student Humanitarian Values." *The Journal of General Education* 54, no. 3 (2005): 237–66. https://doi.org/10.1353/JGE.2006.0004.

Honoré, Carl. "In Praise of Slow Sex." Slow Aging, 2011. https://slowaging.org/praise-slow-sex/.

Hopwood, Christopher J., Evan W. Good, Alytia A. Levendosky, Johannes Zimmermann, Daniela Dumat, Eli J. Finkel, Paul E. Eastwick, and Wiebke Bleidorn. "Realness Is a Core Feature of Authenticity." *Journal of Research in Personality* 92 (2021): 104086. https://doi.org/10.1016/J.JRP.2021.104086.

Horowitz, Gail, Laura A. Rabin, and Donald L. Brodale. "Improving Student Performance in Organic Chemistry: Help Seeking Behaviors and Prior Chemistry Aptitude." *Journal of the Scholarship of Teaching and Learning* 13, no. 3 (2013): 120–33.

Hough, Lynn H. "The Sunday School Lesson." *The Christian Advocate* 95 (1920): 266.

Howitz, William J., Kate J. McKnelly, and Renee D. Link. "Developing and Implementing a Specifications Grading System in an Organic Chemistry Laboratory Course." *Journal of Chemical Education* 98, no. 2 (2021): 385–94.

https://doi.org/10.1021/ACS.JCHEMED.0C00450/SUPPL_FILE/ED0C00450_SI_002.XLSX.

Iacoboni, Marco. "Imitation, Empathy, and Mirror Neurons." *Annual Review of Psychology* 60 (2008): 653–70. https://doi.org/10.1146/ANNUREV.PSYCH.60.110707.163604.

ildan, Mehmet Murat. "Quotes and Quotations of Mehmet Murat Ildan." Mehmet Murat ildan. n.d. muratildanquotations.wordpress.com/2014/05/01/quotes-and-quotations-of-mehmet-murat-ildan-40/.

Ingram, Rick E., and Philip C. Kendall. "The Cognitive Side of Anxiety." *Cognitive Therapy and Research* 11, no. 5 (1987): 523–36. https://doi.org/10.1007/BF01183856.

Jacobs, Robert, Dave Truesdale, and Bob Wayne. "Ray Bradbury Interview." *Tangent #5*, 1976.

Jagger, Mick, and Keith Richards. "You Can't Always Get What You Want." *Let It Bleed*, 1969.

Kaczkurkin, Antonia N., and Edna B. Foa. "Cognitive-Behavioral Therapy for Anxiety Disorders: An Update on the Empirical Evidence." *Dialogues in Clinical Neuroscience* 17, no. 3 (2015): 337. https://doi.org/10.31887/DCNS.2015.17.3/AKACZKURKIN.

Karabenick, Stuart A., and Myron H. Dembo. "Understanding and Facilitating Self-Regulated Help Seeking." *New Directions for Teaching and Learning* 126 (2011): 33–43. https://doi.org/10.1002/TL.442.

Kashdan, Todd B., and William E. Breen. "Materialism and Diminished Well-Being: Experiential Avoidance as a Mediating Mechanism." *Journal of Social and Clinical Psychology* 26, no. 5 (2007): 521–39. https://doi.org/10.1521/JSCP.2007.26.5.521.

Kaul, Vivek. "Sheena Iyengar on 'The Art of Choosing.'" *The Economic Times*, 2011.

Keinan, Anat, Silvia Bellezza, and Neeru Paharia. "The Symbolic Value of Time." *Current Opinion in Psychology* 26 (2019): 58–61. https://doi.org/10.1016/J.COPSYC.2018.05.001.

Keith, Timothy Z., Sheila M. Pottebaum, and Steve Eberhart. "Effects of Self-Concept and Locus of Control on Academic Achievement: A Large-Sample Path Analysis." *Journal of Psychoeducational Assessment* 4, no. 1 (1986): 61–72. https://doi.org/10.1177/073428298600400107.

Kerfoot, Karlene. "Beyond Busyness: Creating Slack in the Organization." *Nursing Economics* 24, no. 3 (2006): 168–70.

Kernis, Michael H., and Brian M. Goldman. "A Multicomponent Conceptualization of Authenticity: Theory and Research." *Advances in*

Experimental Social Psychology 38 (2006): 283–357. https://doi.org/10.1016/S0065-2601(06)38006-9.

Khalaila, Rabia. "The Relationship between Academic Self-Concept, Intrinsic Motivation, Test Anxiety, and Academic Achievement among Nursing Students: Mediating and Moderating Effects." *Nurse Education Today* 35, no. 3 (2015): 432–38. https://doi.org/10.1016/J.NEDT.2014.11.001.

Kidd, Chip. *The Cheese Monkeys: A Novel in Two Semesters*. New York: Scribner, 2001.

Kierkegaard, Søren, Howard Vincent Hong, and Edna Hatlestad Hong. *The Sickness unto Death: A Christian Psychological Exposition for Upbuilding and Awakening*. Princeton, NJ: Princeton University Press, 1980.

Kirkpatrick, Michael A., Kathryn Stant, Shonta Downes, and Leatah Gaither. "Perceived Locus of Control and Academic Performance: Broadening the Construct's Applicability." *Journal of College Student Development* 49, no. 5 (2008): 486–96. https://doi.org/10.1353/CSD.0.0032.

Knippen, Jay T., and Thad B. Green. "Asking for Positive Reinforcement." *Journal of Workplace Learning* 9, no. 5 (1997): 163–68. https://doi.org/10.1108/13665629710169620/FULL/PDF.

Krogerus, Mikael, Roman Tschäppeler, and Jenny Piening. *The Decision Book: Fifty Models for Strategic Thinking*. New York: W. W. Norton, 2012.

Krumrei-Mancuso, Elizabeth J., Fred B. Newton, Eunhee Kim, and Dan Wilcox. "Psychosocial Factors Predicting First-Year College Student Success." *Journal of College Student Development* 54, no. 3 (2013): 247–66. https://doi.org/10.1353/CSD.2013.0034.

Laertius, Diogenes. *Lives of the Eminent Philosophers*. Trans. Pamela Mensch. New York: Oxford University Press, 2018.

Lane, Joel A. "Attachment, Well-Being, and College Senior Concerns about the Transition out of College." *Journal of College Counseling* 19, no. 3 (2016): 231–45. https://doi.org/10.1002/JOCC.12046.

Lawrence, Jerome, and Robert Edwin Lee. *The Night Thoreau Spent in Jail*. New York: Farrar, Straus and Giroux, 2001.

Lemme, Barbara Hansen. *Development in Adulthood*. Prentice Hall, 1999.

Lin, Yi Guang, Wilbert J. McKeachie, and Yung Che Kim. "College Student Intrinsic and/or Extrinsic Motivation and Learning." *Learning and Individual Differences* 13, no. 3 (2003): 251–58. https://doi.org/10.1016/S1041-6080(02)00092-4.

Lyubomirsky, Sonja, Laura King, and Ed Diener. "The Benefits of Frequent Positive Affect: Does Happiness Lead to Success?" *Psychological Bulletin* 131, no. 6 (2005): 803–55. https://doi.org/10.1037/0033-2909.131.6.803.

Mallery, Susan. *Sweet Trouble*. HQN, 2008.
Maraboli, Steve. *Life, the Truth, and Being Free*. A Better Today, 2009.
Marcus Aurelius. *Meditations*. Translated by Robin Hard. Oxford University Press, 2011.
Mau, W.-C., R. Hitchcock, and C. Calvert. "High School Students' Career Plans: The Influence of Others' Expectations." *Professional School Counseling* (1998): 161–66.
Mehta, Poonam. "Authenticity and Employee Wellbeing with Reference to Emotional Work: A Review." *Mental Health and Social Inclusion* 25, no. 2 (2020): 146–58. https://doi.org/10.1108/MHSI-11-2020-0077/FULL/XML.
Miceli, Maria, and Cristiano Castelfranchi. "Nature and Mechanisms of Loss of Motivation," *Review of General Psychology* 4, no. 3 (2000): 238–63. https://doi.org/10.1037/1089-2680.4.3.238.
Miles, Andrew, and Catherine Yeh. "Do Demographic Predictors of Personal Values Vary by Context? A Test of Schwartz's Value Development Theory." *Social Sciences & Humanities Open* 5, no. 1 (2022): 100264. https://doi.org/10.1016/J.SSAHO.2022.100264.
Miller, George A. "The Magical Number Seven, Plus or Minus Two: Some Limits on Our Capacity for Processing Information." *Psychological Review* 63, no. 2 (1956): 81–97. https://doi.org/10.1037/H0043158.
Miller, William, Patrick Miller, and William Hermanns. "Death of a Genius." *LIFE Magazine* 38, no. 18 (1955).
Miloyan, Beyon, Nancy A. Pachana, and Thomas Suddendorf. "The Future Is Here: A Review of Foresight Systems in Anxiety and Depression." *Cognition and Emotion* 28, no. 5 (2014): 795–810. https://doi.org/10.1080/02699931.2013.863179.
Milyavskaya, Marina, Mark Saffran, Nora Hope, and Richard Koestner. "Fear of Missing Out: Prevalence, Dynamics, and Consequences of Experiencing FOMO." *Motivation and Emotion* 42, no. 5 (2018): 725–37. https://doi.org/10.1007/S11031-018-9683-5/TABLES/3.
Moran, Chelsea, Christina Tomei, Monique Lefebvre, Cheryl Harris, Christine Maheu, and Sophie Lebel. "An Exploratory Study of the Worst-Case Scenario Exercise as an Exposure Treatment for Fear of Cancer Recurrence." *Supportive Care in Cancer* 25, no. 5 (2017): 1373–75. https://doi.org/10.1007/S00520-017-3600-4.
Morrison, Toni. *Beloved: A Novel*. New York: Vintage, 2004.
Moyer, John. "A Conversation with César Chávez." *Journal of Current Social Issues* 9, no. 3 (1970).

Najmi, Sadia, Bradley C. Riemann, and Daniel M. Wegner. "Managing Unwanted Intrusive Thoughts in Obsessive-Compulsive Disorder: Relative Effectiveness of Suppression, Focused Distraction, and Acceptance." *Behaviour Research and Therapy* 47, no. 6 (2009): 494–503. https://doi.org/10.1016/J.BRAT.2009.02.015.

Nawa, Norberto Eiji, and Noriko Yamagishi. "Enhanced Academic Motivation in University Students Following a 2-Week Online Gratitude Journal Intervention." *BMC Psychology* 9, no. 1 (2021): 1–16. https://doi.org/10.1186/S40359-021-00559-W/TABLES/5.

Nhat Hanh, Thich. *The Art of Mindfulness*. New York: HarperCollins, 2012.

Owens, Jesse, and Paul G. Neimark. *Jesse, a Spiritual Autobiography*. Logos International, 1978.

Palmer, Amanda, and Brené Brown. *The Art of Asking, or, How I Learned to Stop Worrying and Let People Help*. New York: Grand Central Publishing, 2015.

Pan, Emily X. R. *The Astonishing Color of After*. New York: Little, Brown, 2019.

Paulos, John Allen. *A Mathematician Plays the Stock Market*. New York: Basic Books, 2003.

Penn, William. *Some Fruits of Solitude*. Kessinger Publishing, 2004.

Peplau, L. A., and D. Perlman. *Loneliness: A Sourcebook of Current Theory, Research and Therapy*. New York: Wiley Interscience, 1982.

Perrone, Lisa, and Margaret H. Vickers. "Life after Graduation as a 'Very Uncomfortable World': An Australian Case Study." *Education and Training* 45, no. 2 (2003): 69–78. https://doi.org/10.1108/00400910310464044/FULL/PDF.

Peters, Ellis. *Fallen into the Pit*. Mysterious Press, 1996.

Pigliucci, Massimo, and Gregory Lopez. *A Handbook for New Stoics: How to Thrive in a World out of Your Control: 52 Week-by-Week Lessons*. The Experiment, 2019.

Plato. *Gorgias*. Translated by Robin Waterfield. Oxford: Oxford University Press, 2008.

———. *Phaedrus*. Translated by Robin Waterfield. Oxford: Oxford University Press, 2009.

Ponzetti, James J. "Loneliness among College Students." *Family Relations* 39, no. 3 (1990): 336. https://doi.org/10.2307/584881.

Powdthavee, Nattavudh, Warn N. Lekfuangfu, and Mark Wooden. "What's the Good of Education on Our Overall Quality of Life? A Simultaneous Equation Model of Education and Life Satisfaction for Australia." *Journal of Behavioral and Experimental Economics* 54 (2015): 10–21. https://doi.org/10.1016/J.SOCEC.2014.11.002.

Przybylski, Andrew K., Kou Murayama, Cody R. Dehaan, and Valerie Gladwell. "Motivational, Emotional, and Behavioral Correlates of Fear of Missing Out." *Computers in Human Behavior* 29, no. 4 (2013): 1841–48. https://doi.org/10.1016/J.CHB.2013.02.014.

Puklek Levpušček, Melita, Victoria Rauch, and Luka Komidar. "Individuation in Relation to Parents as a Predictor of Career Goals and Career Optimism in Emerging Adults." *Scandinavian Journal of Psychology* 59, no. 2 (2018): 146–56. https://doi.org/10.1111/SJOP.12421.

Quayhagen, M. P., and M. Quayhagen. "Alzheimer's Stress: Coping with the Caregiving Role." *The Gerontologist* 28, no. 3 (1988): 391–96. https://doi.org/10.1093/GERONT/28.3.391.

Ratna, Abhishek. *Small Wins BIG SUCCESS: A Handbook for Exemplary Success in Post Covid19 Outbreak Era.* Abhishek Ratna, 2020.

Ray, William J., and Meredith Faith. "Dissociative Experiences in a College Age Population: Follow-up with 1190 Subjects." *Personality and Individual Differences* 18, no. 2 (1995): 223–30. https://doi.org/10.1016/0191-8869(94)00137-H.

Richardson, Helen M. "Community of Values as a Factor in Friendships of College and Adult Women." *Journal of Social Psychology* 11, no. 2 (1940): 303–12. https://doi.org/10.1080/00224545.1940.9918751.

Robertson, Donald. *How to Think Like a Roman Emperor: The Stoic Philosophy of Marcus Aurelius.* New York: St. Martin's, 2019.

Robison, Jennifer. "Are You Happy Now?" *Gallup Business Journal*, February 5, 2005.

Rogers, Carl Ransom. *On Becoming a Person: A Therapist's View of Psychotherapy.* New York: HarperOne, 1995.

Romakkaniemi, Marjo, and Arja Kilpeläinen. "The Meaningful Elements in Recovering from Major Depression as a Basis of Developing Social Work in Mental Health Services." *Social Work in Mental Health* 13, no. 5 (2015): 439–58. https://doi.org/10.1080/15332985.2014.932317.

Rosner, Brian S. *The Consolations of Theology.* Grand Rapids, MI: William B. Eerdmans, 2008.

Rothman, Miriam, and Ruth Sisman. "Internship Impact on Career Consideration among Business Students." *Education and Training* 58, no. 9 (2016): 1003–13. https://doi.org/10.1108/ET-04-2015-0027/FULL/PDF.

Roulin, Nicolas, and Adrian Bangerter. "Extracurricular Activities in Young Applicants' Résumés: What Are the Motives behind Their Involvement?" *International Journal of Psychology* 48, no. 5 (2013): 871–80. https://doi.org/10.1080/00207594.2012.692793.

Rowa, K. "Atychiphobia (Fear of Failure)." In *Phobias: The Psychology of Irrational Fear*, edited by Irena Milosevic and Randi E. McCabe. Santa Barbara, CA: Greenwood, 2015.

Russell, Jack, Barbara Russell, and William J. Tastle. "Teaching Soft Skills in a Systems Development Capstone Class." *Information Systems Education Journal* 3, no. 19 (2005).

Sagiv, Lilach, Sonia Roccas, Jan Cieciuch, and Shalom H. Schwartz. "Personal Values in Human Life." *Nature Human Behaviour* 1, no. 9 (2017): 630–39. https://doi.org/10.1038/s41562-017-0185-3.

Schnoes, Alexandra M., Anne Caliendo, Janice Morand, Teresa Dillinger, Michelle Naffziger-Hirsch, Bruce Moses, Jeffery C. Gibeling, Keith R. Yamamoto, Bill Lindstaedt, Richard McGee, and Theresa C. O'Brien. "Internship Experiences Contribute to Confident Career Decision Making for Doctoral Students in the Life Sciences." *CBE Life Sciences Education* 17, no. 1 (2018): 16. https://doi.org/10.1187/CBE.17-08-0164/ASSET/IMAGES/LARGE/CBE-17-AR16-G003.JPEG.

Schriver, Jennifer, and Nicole Teske. "Anticipating College Graduation: The Concerns and Coping Methods of College Seniors." *Journal of the First-Year Experience and Students in Transition* 32, no. 1 (2020): 79–95.

Schunk, D. H., and B. J. Zimmerman. *Self-Regulation of Learning and Performance: Issues and Educational Applications*. Hillsdale, NJ: Lawrence Erlbaum, 1994.

Schunk, Dale H. "Goal Setting and Self-Efficacy during Self-Regulated Learning." *Educational Psychologist* 25, no. 1 (1990): 71–86. https://doi.org/10.1207/S15326985EP2501_6.

Schunk, Dale H., and Antoinette R. Hanson. "Influence on Children's Self-Efficacy and Achievement." *Journal of Educational Psychology* 77, no. 3 (1985): 313–22. https://doi.org/10.1037/0022-0663.77.3.313.

Seligman, Martin E. P. *Authentic Happiness: Using the New Positive Psychology to Realize Your Potential for Lasting Fulfillment*. New York: Free Press, 2002.

Seneca, Lucius Annaeus. *Anger, Mercy, Revenge—The Complete Works of Lucius Annaeus Seneca*. Translated by Robert A. Kaster and Martha C. Nussbaum. Chicago: University of Chicago Press, 2010.

———. *Hardship and Happiness*. Translated by Elaine Fathom, Harry M. Hine, James Ker, and Gareth D. Williams. Chicago: University of Chicago Press, 2016.

———. *Hercules Oetaeus (Hercules on Mount Oeta)*. Translated by Frank Justus Miller. Morrisville, NC: Lulu Press, 2021.

———. *Letters from a Stoic*. Translated by Coralie Bickford-Smith and Robin Campbell. London: Penguin Classics, 2015.
———. *Letters on Ethics: To Lucilius*. Translated by Margaret Graver and A. A. Long. Chicago: University of Chicago Press, 2015.
———. *Moral Letters to Lucilius—Letters from a Stoic*. Translated by Richard M. Gummere. Cambridge, MA: Loeb Classical Library Edition, 1915.
———. *On the Shortness of Life*. Translated by John W. Basore. Vigeo Press, 2016.
Shakespeare, William. *Hamlet*. Edited by Sylvan Barnet. New York: Signet, 1998.
Shields, Stephanie A. *Speaking from the Heart: Gender and the Social Meaning of Emotion*. Cambridge: Cambridge University Press, 2002.
Shimkunas, Algimantas M. "Anxiety and Expectancy Change: The Effects of Failure and Uncertainty." *Journal of Personality and Social Psychology* 15, no. 1 (1970): 34–42. https://doi.org/10.1037/H0029216.
Silver, Blake R., and Josipa Roksa. "Navigating Uncertainty and Responsibility: Understanding Inequality in the Senior-Year Transition." *Journal of Student Affairs Research and Practice* 54, no. 3 (2017): 248–60. https://doi.org/10.10 80/19496591.2017.1331851.
Simmons, R. G., F. Rosenberg, and M. Rosenberg. "Disturbance in the Self-Image at Adolescence." *American Sociological Review* 38, no. 5 (1973): 553–68. https://doi.org/10.2307/2094407.
Simons, Jeffrey S., Thomas A. Wills, Noah N. Emery, and Philip J. Spelman. "Keep Calm and Carry On: Maintaining Self-Control When Intoxicated, Upset, or Depleted." *Cognition and Emotion* 30, no. 8 (2016): 1415–29. https://doi.org/10.1080/02699931.2015.1069733.
Simons, Joke, Siegfried Dewitte, and Willy Lens. "The Role of Different Types of Instrumentality in Motivation, Study Strategies, and Performance: Know Why You Learn, So You'll Know What You Learn!" *British Journal of Educational Psychology* 74, no. 3 (2004): 343–60. https://doi.org/10.1348/0007099041552314.
Sinek, Simon (@simonsinek). Twitter. 2021. https://twitter.com/simonsinek/status/1366414716042625025?.
Spinath, Birgit, and Ricarda Steinmayr. "The Roles of Competence Beliefs and Goal Orientations for Change in Intrinsic Motivation." *Journal of Educational Psychology* 104, no. 4 (2012): 1135–48. https://doi.org/10.1037/A0028115.

Stahl, Ashley. "Six Reasons Why Your College Major Doesn't Matter." *Forbes*, August 12, 2015. www.forbes.com/sites/ashleystahl/2015/08/12/six-reasons-why-your-college-major-doesnt-matter/.

Statius. *Thebaid*. Edited and translated by D. R. Shackleton Bailey. Vol. 2. Cambridge, MA: Harvard University Press, 2004.

Stewart, Graeme, Tricia Anne Seifert, and Carol Rolheiser. "Anxiety and Self-Efficacy's Relationship with Undergraduate Students' Perceptions of the Use of Metacognitive Writing Strategies." *The Canadian Journal for the Scholarship of Teaching and Learning* 6, no. 1 (March 31, 2015). https://doi.org/10.5206/CJSOTL-RCACEA.2015.1.4.

Strickland, David, and Carol Strickland. "My Sociology: The Challenge of Transforming Classroom Culture from a Focus on Grades to a Focus on Learning." *The Journal of Public and Professional Sociology* 5, no. 2 (2013).

Suhre, Cor J. M., Ellen P. W. A. Jansen, and Egbert G. Harskamp. "Impact of Degree Program Satisfaction on the Persistence of College Students." *Higher Education* 54, no. 2 (2006): 207–26. https://doi.org/10.1007/S10734-005-2376-5.

Swain, J. R. L. "The Nature and Assessment of Scientific Explorations in the Classroom." *School Science Review* 72, no. 260 (1991): 65–77.

Swanson, Christopher B. "Spending Time or Investing Time? Involvement in High School Curricular and Extracurricular Activities as Strategic Action." *Rationality and Society* 14, no. 4 (2002): 431–71. https://doi.org/10.1177/1043463102014004002.

Syrus, Publilius. *The Moral Sayings of Publilius Syrus: A Roman Slave*. Translated by Darius Lyman. Kessinger, 2010.

Telch, Michael J., David P. Valentiner, Doron Ilai, Paula R. Young, Mark B. Powers, and Jasper A. J. Smits. "Fear Activation and Distraction during the Emotional Processing of Claustrophobic Fear." *Journal of Behavior Therapy and Experimental Psychiatry* 35, no. 3 (2004): 219–32. https://doi.org/10.1016/J.JBTEP.2004.03.004.

Tice, Dianne M. "The Social Motivations of People with Low Self-Esteem." In *Self-Esteem: The Plenum Series in Social/Clinical Psychology*, edited by R. F. Baumeister, 37–53. Boston: Springer, 1993. https://doi.org/10.1007/978-1-4684-8956-9_3.

Tieu, Thanh-Thanh, and S. Mark Pancer. "Cocurricular Involvement and First-Year Students' Transition to University: Quality vs. Quantity of Involvement." *Journal of The First-Year Experience and Students in Transition* 21, no. 1 (2009): 43–63.

Tobias, Sigmund. "Anxiety and Cognitive Processing of Instruction." In *Self-Related Cognitions in Anxiety and Motivation*, edited by Ralf Schwarzer. Psychology Press, 1986.

Tolkien, J. R. R. *The Fellowship of the Ring: Being the First Part of The Lord of the Rings*. New York: Ballantine Books, 1997.

Tolle, Eckhart. *A New Earth: Awakening to Your Life's Purpose*. New York: Dutton/Penguin Group, 2005.

Travers, Cheryl J., Dominique Morisano, and Edwin A. Locke. "Self-Reflection, Growth Goals, and Academic Outcomes: A Qualitative Study." *British Journal of Educational Psychology* 85, no. 2 (2015): 224–41. https://doi.org/10.1111/BJEP.12059.

Trevino, Naomi Noel, and Stacie Craft DeFreitas. "The Relationship between Intrinsic Motivation and Academic Achievement for First Generation Latino College Students." *Social Psychology of Education* 17, no. 2 (2014): 293–306. https://doi.org/10.1007/S11218-013-9245-3/TABLES/2.

"U.S. Census Bureau Releases New Educational Attainment Data." Washington, DC: US Census, 2020.

Valdovinos, Maria G. "The Impact of a Year-Long Service-Learning Experience on Student Perception of Ability to Conduct Functional Assessments." *Scholarship of Teaching and Learning in Psychology* 2, no. 2 (2016): 125–33. https://doi.org/10.1037/STL0000058.

Vasey, Michael W., and Thomas D. Borkovec. "A Catastrophizing Assessment of Worrisome Thoughts." *Cognitive Therapy and Research* 16, no. 5 (1992): 505–20. https://doi.org/10.1007/BF01175138.

Vespia, Kristin M., Georjeanna Wilson-Doenges, Ryan C. Martin, and Deirdre M. Radosevich. "Experiential Learning." In *Evidence-Based Teaching for Higher Education*, edited by B. M. Schwartz and R. A. R. Gurung, 97. Washington, DC: American Psychological Association, 2012. https://doi.org/10.1037/13745-005.

Vitterso, Joar, and Yngvil Søholt. "Life Satisfaction Goes with Pleasure and Personal Growth Goes with Interest: Further Arguments for Separating Hedonic and Eudaimonic Well-Being." *The Journal of Positive Psychology* 6, no. 4 (2011): 326–35. https://doi.org/10.1080/17439760.2011.584548.

Wahl, Kay Herting, and Anne Blackhurst. "Factors Affecting the Occupational and Educational Aspirations of Children and Adolescents." *Professional School Counseling* 3, no. 5 (2000): 367.

Walter Winchell. "Walter Winchell on Broadway." *Logansport Pharos-Tribune*, January 26, 1939.

Washington, George. *The Writings of George Washington: Official Letters Relating to the French War, and Private Letters before the American Revolution: March, 1754–May, 1775*. Edited by Jared Sparks. Nabu Press, 2011.

Weinstein, Maxine, and Meredith A. Lane. *Sociality, Hierarchy, Health: Comparative Biodemography: A Collection of Papers* (Washington, DC: The National Academies Press, 2014). https://doi.org/10.17226/18822.

West, Thomas G., and Grace Starry West. *Four Texts on Socrates: Plato's Euthyphro, Apology, and Crito, and Aristophanes' Clouds*. Ithaca, NY: Cornell University Press, 1998.

Wheeler, Ladd, Harry Reis, and John B. Nezlek. "Loneliness, Social Interaction, and Sex Roles." *Journal of Personality and Social Psychology* 45, no. 4 (1983): 943–53. https://doi.org/10.1037/0022-3514.45.4.943.

Wilde, Oscar. *De Profundis*. Ægypan Press, 2006.

Williams, Chris, and Anne Garland. "Identifying and Challenging Unhelpful Thinking." *Advances in Psychiatric Treatment* 8, no. 5 (2002): 377–86. https://doi.org/10.1192/APT.8.5.377.

Wilson, Timothy D., David A. Reinhard, Erin C. Westgate, Daniel T. Gilbert, Nicole Ellerbeck, Cheryl Hahn, Casey L. Brown, and Adi Shaked. "Just Think: The Challenges of the Disengaged Mind." *Science* 345, no. 6192 (2014): 75–77. https://doi.org/10.1126/SCIENCE.1250830.

Wilt, Joshua, Wiebke Bleidorn, and William Revelle. "Finding a Life Worth Living: Meaning in Life and Graduation from College." *European Journal of Personality* 30, no. 2 (2016): 158–67. https://doi.org/10.1002/per.2046.

Winchester, Jesse. "Do It." Toronto: Eastern Sound, 1972.

Wine, Jeri. "Test Anxiety and Direction of Attention." *Psychological Bulletin* 76, no. 2 (1971): 92–104. https://doi.org/10.1037/H0031332.

Winkle-Wagner, Rachelle, Carmen M. McCallum, Courtney Luedke, and Brittany Ota-Malloy. "Instrumental or Meaningful Friendships: Black Alumnae Perspectives on Peer Relationships during College." *Journal of Women and Gender in Higher Education* 12, no. 3 (2019): 283–98. https://doi.org/10.1080/19407882.2019.1593201.

Witter, Robert A., Morris A. Okun, William A. Stock, and Marilyn J. Haring. "Education and Subjective Well-Being: A Meta-Analysis." *Educational Evaluation and Policy Analysis* 6, no. 2 (1984): 165–73. https://doi.org/10.3102/01623737006002165.

Wittmaier, Bruce C. "Test Anxiety and Study Habits." *The Journal of Educational Research* 65, no. 8 (1972): 352–54. https://doi.org/10.1080/00220671.1972.10884344.

Woolfolk, Ann. "Toshiko Takaezu." *Princeton Alumni Weekly* 83, no. 5 (1982): 31–33.

Wright, Robin Redmon. "Real Men Don't Ask for Directions: Male Student Attitudes toward Peer Tutoring." *Journal of College Reading and Learning* 34, no. 1 (2003): 61–75. https://doi.org/10.1080/10790195.2003.10850156.

Wrzesniewski, Amy, Barry Schwartz, Xiangyu Cong, Michael Kane, Audrey Omar, and Thomas Kolditz. "Multiple Types of Motives Don't Multiply the Motivation of West Point Cadets." *Proceedings of the National Academy of Sciences of the United States of America* 111, no. 30 (2014): 10990–95. https://doi.org/10.1073/PNAS.1405298111/SUPPL_FILE/PNAS.201405298SI.PDF.

Yanguas, Javier, Sacramento Pinazo-Henandis, and Francisco José Tarazona-Santabalbina. "The Complexity of Loneliness." *Acta Bio Medica: Atenei Parmensis* 89, no. 2 (2018): 302. https://doi.org/10.23750/ABM.V89I2.7404.

Yazedjian, Ani, Becki Kielaszek, and Michelle Toews. "Students' Perceptions Regarding Their Impending Transition out of College." *Journal of The First-Year Experience and Students in Transition* 22, no. 2 (2010): 33–48.

Zwemer, Weare A., and Jerry L. Deffenbacher. "Irrational Beliefs, Anger, and Anxiety." *Journal of Counseling Psychology* 31, no. 3 (1984): 391–93. https://doi.org/10.1037/0022-0167.31.3.391.

INDEX

Aesop's Fables, 30
aims. *See* goals
Antoninus, Marcus Aurelius, 9, 40, 50, 58, 77, 141, 153
anxiety, effects of, 24–25, 41–46, 51, 58, 62, 65–73, 85, 93, 95, 99, 145–147
appraisal. *See* judgements from others

Bader-Ginsburg, Ruth, 142
boaster. *See* impressing others
bragging. *See* impressing others
burnout, 124

catastrophizing, 51, 65–71
coerce. *See* external pressure
compliments. *See* praise
Confucius, 83–84
control, effects on anxiety, 6, 12, 40–44, 62, 68, 85–86, 92–94, 97, 124, 127, 140–141, 150–151, 157–161
core identity, 10–12, 17, 139
core values, 12–16, 30, 32, 52, 116, 119, 150–151, 159–160
criticism, 4, 11–15, 39, 41, 139–141, 144–145

Dalai Lama, 141
Dante Alighieri, 1
decision making, 2, 4–7, 11, 13–15, 22, 33–37, 42, 104–108, 114–115, 118–119, 132–134, 136–137, 159
disappointing others, fear of, 3, 65, 111, 140–142
disapproval. *See* criticism
distractions, 20, 50–54, 57–58, 68, 104
Duckworth, Angela, vii, 156

embarrassment, fear of, 19, 21–27, 65
Emerson, Ralph Waldo, 113
emotional distance, 16–17, 69, 72
emotional reactions, 14–15, 24, 34, 36, 58, 70–72, 87, 93, 96, 117, 137, 144, 146,
Epictetus, 32, 44, 75, 153
external pressure (family/peers/community), x, 2–7, 102–105, 118, 134, 140–141, 147–148

failure, 2, 4, 21, 99, 112, 119
fear of missing out (FOMO), 19–21, 23–26, 49, 106

Ferriss, Timothy, 76, 94
Franklin, Benjamin, 102, 121
fraud. *See* imposter

genuine social connections. *See* loneliness
goal-oriented. *See* outcome-oriented
goals, 3, 32, 35, 41–43, 46–47, 52, 54, 93–95, 97–99, 124–126; re-evaluation, 2, 5, 7, 13, 44, 62–63, 112–119, 149–150

Hillesum, Etty, 20
Holiday, Ryan, 155
human evolution, 11–12, 31, 34, 76, 144

implementation intention, 54
imposter, 113
impressing others, 9, 42–43, 52, 86, 129–134
incompetent. *See* failure
indecision. *See* uncertainty
intrinsic vs. extrinsic motivators, 4–5, 7, 40–47, 54, 104, 150, 158–161

judgments from others, perception of, 4, 14–15, 17, 22, 27, 34, 68, 86–87, 140, 143–147

Kierkegaard, Søren, 1

Laertius, Diogenes, xi
letters of advice, 15, 26, 37, 72, 106
loneliness, 29–34, 36–38

Morrison, Toni, 10

negative thought spirals. *See* catastrophizing
nervousness. *See* anxiety

objectives. *See* goals
ostracize. *See* rejection
outcast. *See* loneliness
outcome-oriented, 5, 34, 36, 40–42, 46, 60, 66–72, 94, 150, 157–158, 161
Owens, Jesse, 132–133

peer comparisons, 68, 76–81, 85, 129, 131, 150
physical sensations associated with emotions, 33–37, 61
Pigliucci, Massimo, 154
plans. *See* goals
Plato, 93, 140
praise, 9–15, 39–40, 75–77
pretentious. *See* impressing others
progress-oriented, 42–43, 46, 99, 150, 161

rumination. *See* catastrophizing
rejection, 19, 33, 35–37, 65, 117, 136
results-oriented. *See* outcome-oriented
résumé, 19, 21, 28, 129–131
Robertson, Donald, 154

self-doubt, 140–143
self-esteem. *See* self-image
self-image, 10–17, 21, 36, 41, 75–76, 85, 111–112
Seligman, Martin, 156
Seneca, Lucius Annaeus, 20, 58, 65, 66, 93, 130, 154

Shakespeare, William, 112
social evolution. *See* human evolution
social media. *See* distractions
sycophant. *See* impressing others

Tolkien, J. R. R., 142

uncertainty, 91–99, 123, 141, 143–145

Varmus, Harold E., 142

Washington, George, 31
worry. *See* anxiety
worst-case scenario, 10, 16, 51, 67, 70–71, 84, 87, 89, 105, 108, 117–118

Zeno, xi

ABOUT THE AUTHOR

Dustin Brisson is a first-generation, low-income college graduate born and raised in California. He earned a bachelor's degree in biology from Pepperdine University and a PhD in ecology and evolution from Stony Brook University. He is a Burrough's Wellcome Fellow and professor in the department of biology at the University of Pennsylvania, where he leads the Evolution and Ecology of Disease Systems Laboratory. His scientific research investigates the ecology (interactions affecting distribution and abundance) and evolution (change in genotype and phenotype due to neutral or selected processes) of disease-causing organisms and their natural host populations, with a particular focus on the Lyme disease system.

Through a combination of personal experiences as a first-generation low-income college student, as a teacher in introductory and non-major biology courses, and acting as a mentor to undergraduates at Penn, he developed a dedicated interest in developing strategies derived from philosophy, psychology, and evolutionary biology to guide students through their college experience and into their careers. Many of these strategies are presented in *In Pursuit of the Good Life*, which is aimed at providing students with the necessary tools to overcome many of the most common issues faced by college students.